ROCK 'n' ROLL MUSIC:
Brixton
Boy
Calling

The Life and Times of Author / Agent / Producer
Peter Harrison
Featuring ... **AMAZING BEATLES CHRONICLE**

- ➤ Led Zeppelin's first ever gig
- ➤ Pink Floyd residency at RCA
- ➤ David Bowie compered 'SEARCH'
- ➤ The Who auditioned as 'High Numbers'
- ➤ Rod Stewart helped save Rock Music Agency
- ➤ Marc Bolan appeared at Mistrale club
- ➤ A history of rock music throughout 1960's

****

ROCK 'n' ROLL MUSIC

Brixton Boy Calling

By Peter Harrison
Copyright c Laurence Peter Binns Harrison 2013

My 1960's Rock Music Roller Coaster ride & the exhilarating ongoing journey

First published 2013

A unique era. Innovation, inspiration and the 'Creative Revolution'.

The right of Laurence Peter Binns Harrison to be identified as author of this work had been asserted in accordance with section 77 and 78 of the Copyright, Designs and Patents Act, 1988

Many thanks to David McEwan for the posters

A CreateSpace publication

ISBN-13: 978-1493596997
10: 1493596993

CONTENTS

INTRO - Rock Music Agent

TRACK 1 - Hard Rock – Hot Sex

#TRACK 2 - The Decade of the Millennium

#TRACK 3 - The Groups

#TRACK 4 - Search - With David Bowie

TRACK 5 - The Children That Time Forgot

#TRACK 6 - Brixton Boy Calling

TRACK 7 - Positive Influences

#INTRO
Rock Music Agent & Touring Producer

It was 1960 and I was the youngest Rock Music Agent in Soho. In those days you had to be 21 to be licenced, the age of majority back then. Westminster City Council sent their Entertainment Employment Agency Inspector [a former policeman] to interview me. He said I was a fit and proper person to be granted a licence. I was a lean keen teenager, aged 19. The agency business was very slow when I began. I started by trying to book groups into local beat clubs. It only became a success when I focused on booking Colleges. I then formed College Entertainments Ltd. I sold it in 1972 after enjoying twelve hectic years on an exciting rock'n'roller coaster ride.

I then became a music and variety touring producer. I had to be so focused as an agent negotiating contracts with hardnosed managers. But this was far more relaxed. Producing shows, dealing with theatre managers and the love of my life by my side.

"MRS. SHUFFLEWICK" - Celebrity Female Impersonator
Resident Star Performer at the Black Cap, CAMDEN for many years.

The start of my life was an explosive affair. A German bomb scored a direct hit on our house at 100 Arodene Road. Brixton Hill. London. SW2 in 1942. Mum was pushing me in my pram through Brixton market at the time of the explosion. If it had been raining, and I had stayed at home, then I would have become a candidate for *the children that time forgot.*

We were homeless, so Mum, dad and baby {me} were moved into a Nissen hut. It was hurriedly built on some waste ground at the bottom of Tulse Hill. A 'Yank' built 'hut' with two bedrooms, cold water and an outside loo. There was no bath and the heat came from an open coal fire.

Not long afterwards tragedy struck again. My mother died of Polio, I was seven.

Children don't realise what they're going through at the time, they just get on with it. Although my mother's death did hit me hard. I was struck dumb for over a month.

But when I recovered I got stuck in to playing about and mucking around. I grew mint and sold it in Arlingford and Brailsford Roads, next to Brockwell Park, for tuppence a bunch. My friends and I played on the many bomb sites scattered around Brixton Hill. We also played football, cricket, conkers and read The Beano. I was a member of the Apache Road gang. We were chucked out of Brixton's Woolworths for not wearing shirts. We were poor enough for me to receive free school dinners all year round, including summer holidays. We always wanted to go to Chalk Farm to collect some chalk. But best of all we kissed all those delightful girls in the Piggery, later to become the Dick Sheppard School.

Lambeth Council told my dad that the hut was only temporary. A long fourteen years later we were moved into Rudhall House on the Tulse Hill Estate. Homeless people have been known to refuse accommodation on that notorious estate.

Any spare money dad made by working in a car and motorbike showroom in Stockwell went on his hobby, greyhound racing.

When my sister and I were young kids we were left outside of these greyhound stadiums for hours on end. I hated it, so boring. We were stuck in the motorbike sidecar with a packet of crisps for company. The dog tracks we waited outside of were Wandsworth and Wimbledon. It reached a lowpoint when I watched a man drop a sackful of kittens into the River Wandle.

Dad was always a caring and loving father to

me and my sister. He fought against us being taken into care. And in spite of the intense pressure put on him, he won through. We stayed together as a family.

I was in the higher grammar stream at school but wanted out. West Norwood Comp was the worst school on earth. It is now some kind of youth centre. A teenager was murdered there recently.

I left school and immediately got a job (It was easier back then) as a runner at ITV, with Associated Rediffusion at TV House, Kingsway. London.

I go into detail about these events later. In the meantime here are some tasty rock h'ordeves to be getting on with before we look at the main menu…

<u>DAVID BOWIE:</u> The legendary David Bowie agreed to be my compere when I was producing a Melody Maker college music competition. It was held at the Lyceum in the Strand. My presentation sponsored by Melody Maker, the up market music paper. 'Search' was a talent competition for up and coming rock groups on the college circuit. We arranged the auditions in colleges throughout the UK. David Bowie organized the final with me. He was a consummate pro. He helped me make the evening a great success.

The after show get together was fascinating. Many new age females attracted to other stunning females. The evening contained an atmosphere of sexual frisson. The excitement was conjured by those evocative young women, no matter their sexual preferences.

I also declare that David is a true SUPER STAR.

LED ZEPPELIN: Back in 1968 their manager, Peter Grant, phoned me and said that because I had been one of his best agents for The Yardbirds I could be the first to book Led Zep. The Yardbirds had played one of their last gigs for me, appropriately enough, in the 'Last Chance Saloon', Oxford Street.

Within the hour of Grant's call I had booked their very first gig, it was at Surrey University. The fee was just a few hundred pounds. Later I mentioned that fee to a social secretary. Grant heard about it and threatened me, 'Never ever reveal it again'.

They became iconic rock legends. Led Zeppelin will live for evermore. Much of it is down to their rough tough shrewd manager, the late Peter Grant.

And to think Peter, in the late 1950's, was the bouncer at the 2i's coffee bar in Old Compton

Street. Before I started my rock music agency I was employed as a representative by a leading Jukebox Company. Because I was a 'music fan - atic' they asked me to select all the records for that big America Wurlitzer Jukebox at the famous 2i's coffee bar in Old Compton Street. O.C.S. is now the hub of London's gay scene.

I often bumped into the large, menacing figure of a young Peter Grant, the 'doorman' at the 2'is. He was also a part time wrestler and friend of Paul, the owner. Peter Grant and I got on fine. But neither of us could have forecast the future. It came to pass that many years later we were doing business together. Him as a manager, me as an agent.

I remember meeting music producer Mickie Most and rock star Gene Vincent at that popular hang out in London's Soho. Mickie divulged his current love interest, at that that time it was a famous film actress.

All this was back in the late 1950's when the venue was well-known due to earlier appearances of Cliff Richard, Tommy Steele and other rising stars. The owner of the famous coffee bar was TV wrestler Paul Lincoln and his manager, the formidable Tom Littlewood. I was in charge of the Wurlitzer Juke Box. I was an eighteen year old teenager and chose the records and collected the money for my boss at Jukebox Distributors Ltd in Wardour Street.

The 2i's had room for about 20 people. There was an espresso machine and a door at the back led to the kitchen. This doubled as Tom's office. Many a time Tom and I counted the considerable amount of cash from the jukebox. Coins from yesteryear, threepenny bit pieces, sixpences and silver shillings. The kitchen/office was cramped so we counted the week's takings on the draining board. We were on a fifty fifty agreement so we counted the coins carefully. No fiddling allowed. We were pressed against the sink and gas cooker. On the wall behind us was a four penny slot telephone with buttons A and B. Press A when they answered or B for your money back.

Tom was always friendly to me. He never objected to the choice of records I selected for his jukebox. His boss Paul was a man of few words. A big brooding TV wrestler whose menacing look spoke volumes. Both boss Paul and manager Tom came from up North. There was a rumour that Tom was an ex-soldier who'd had had a rough time in the services. Although he was a celebrity in that famous music venue it didn't seem to interest him.

The usual clientele included many Rock and Roll hopefuls. They were always giving me advice about which new releases to choose for the famous jukebox. I always chose my own favourites. They must have been very good choices because the jukebox played non-stop. To Tom it was just another income stream.

On the walls of the 2i's were many photos of musicians who had played there. Being a starry-eyed teenager, I gloried in the show biz atmosphere of this world famous coffee bar. It was featured in the film 'The Tommy Steele Story'. Cliff Richard and the Drifters (The Shadows) played there before they were famous. And the BBC once did a programme about the hand-jive craze, with some teenagers sitting in rows downstairs. Tom Littlewood put on 'entertainment' in that basement, and charged people to go in.

My job was also to select all the records for most of the other major coffee bars throughout Soho. This included the famous 'Heaven & Hell' coffee bar next door to the 2i's. I had acquired a wide range of musical knowledge about new releases and the 'Hit Parade'. I also picked modern jazz records for the beatnik's favourite place, Sam Widges in Berwick Street. The MJQ (Modern Jazz Quartet) were the preferred choice for that crowd. It was a job I thoroughly enjoyed just prior to opening my new rock music agency.

PINK FLOYD: I am proud and privileged to have booked the *original* Pink Floyd for those resident gigs at the Royal College of Art Students Union, Kensington Gore. Many of the female students fancied the sexy Pink Floyd boys. And famous painter David Hockney, a student at RCA at the time, bopped to Pink Floyd. They featured a light show at that time.

Lead singer / Composer Syd Barrett eventually 'retired'; he sadly passed away in July 2006 aged 60. Gone but never forgotten. David Gilmour replaced Syd Barrett in April 1968.

As I write this I am playing Dave Gilmour's 'Live in Gdansk' CD. It is brilliant. Paul, my eldest son, bought it for my birthday.

I particularly like tracks 5 – 'Echoes'.
And track 8 – 'Comfortably Numb'.

MARC BOLAN / T REX: I booked Marc as a solo performer for a gig at the Mistrale club in Beckenham.
While I was talking to Marc I got a profound sense of loneliness and a touch of sadness. Was I picking up vibrations for his current state? Or for the future tragedy? I will never know. Marc Bolan - born Mark Feld; 30 September 1947 – Died 16 September 1977. The cause? The car he was in smashed into a

tree, driven by his girlfriend.

Marc was an English singer-songwriter, guitarist and poet. Marc was not only the founder, front man, lead singer & guitarist for T. Rex, but also a successful solo artist. His music, as well as his original sense of style, helped create the glam rock era. Marc was highly talented and had so much more to offer.

THE WHO: They first came into my life as The High Numbers soon after I had opened my first agency. Trying to get Star Attractions off the ground was a real challenge. Thank goodness that College Ents was an instant and runaway success. I was in the right place and the right time when the Social Secretaries had big budgets to spend.

When I started out I took over the former jazz club, known as Cy Laurie's, in Ham Yard, Great Windmill Street, Piccadilly. I renamed it 'The King Creole Club' after the Elvis film. I was holding auditions for a resident group and The Who (High Numbers) were candidates.

They were typical no nonsense Mods. When they jumped out of their van they told me they had to be nippy. They were so fast in setting up that they were playing their first number within minutes of arriving. No fucking with

The Who. Their 1960's attitude was right in your face. 'Do you want us or not, Pete? Don't fuck us about, we're the new kids on the block, we need an instant decision.'

So they played the audition set and were gone as quickly as they had arrived. Whoosh!
I met the group years later at a gig I arranged for them at the London College of Printing at the Elephant & Castle. They really did destroy their instruments. Neither the students nor I could believe what we were witnessing. What a waste of expensive instruments BUT worth a ton in publicity.

ERIC CLAPTON: I booked this superstar many times. In the early to mid-sixties he was always leaving one group and joining another on a regular basis. We now know that he was searching for that perfect 'blues' sound. His first band was called The Roosters back in 1963.

They were around for a short time before he joined Casey Jones and the Engineers. I first booked Eric in those bands, he then replaced Anthony 'Top' Topham in the Yardbirds. Then went on to become part of John Mayall & the Bluesbreakers. In his one-year stay with Mayall, Clapton gained the nickname "Slowhand" and graffiti in London declared, "Clapton is God."

THE EQUALS WITH EDDY GRANT: The group were made up of equal white and black musicians, hence The Equals. I got this excellent group a well-paid gig at a college. They had a really good sound and became spectacularly successful with many hits.

But I did not like the attitude of the group's leader Eddy Grant towards me. I went over to say hello and he gave me the rudest cold shoulder. I resented his attitude. Grant was treating me like I was a white cop stopping him in his flash expensive motor.

What a contrast to the love I felt from Jamaican Desmond Dekker who had a No 1 hit with 'Israelites'. He always gave me a great big warm West Indian hug whenever we met.

ROD STEWART Rod started recording for Decca and released "Good Morning Little Schoolgirl" in 1964. At that time he was working with a rock'n'blues combo. Rod worked for me at a regular Tuesday night gig at La Discotheque in Wardour Street. He played many of the London beat clubs during this period. I booked Rod on many occasions including when he was featured with Jimmy Powell and the Dimensions. Rod was also a vocalist in John Baldry's 'Hoochie Coochie Men'. They played at many of my college gigs. It was Rod who fronted the group with John that saved my music agency back in 1967.

THANK YOU ROD.
BILL HAYLEY

I even booked the granddaddy of rock'n'roll. Bill Hayley and his Comets. Bill was a farmer's boy who started out playing hillbilly music at county fairs. Bill released 'Candy Kisses' aged 18 in 1945.

Hayley later recorded 'Rocket 88' which was accepted as the first ever rock'n'roll hit record, released in 1951.

In 1954 Bill Hayley moved from Essex records to Decca. Bill recorded that all time rock'n'roll hit 'Rock Around The Clock' which was promoted via the feature film, 'The Blackboard Jungle'. Bill's big hit went to number 1 in both the UK and the USA.

I was slightly disappointed when I met my rock'n'roll idol. Bill Hayley was by then a maturing rock legend and was a little bloated and overweight.

I felt a little odd when I greeted him and looked him in the eyes. He looked straight at me but his eyes were a bit *skee wiff.* He was a slightly boss eyed and his 'kiss curl' was fading fast. But that did not stop me enjoying his performance.

Bill Hayley was one of the biggest names my company, Star Attractions Ltd, had booked. The gig was a great success at the Mistrale club in Beckenham in Kent.

MISTRALE CLUB
2-4 HIGH STREET, BECKENHAM, KENT
FORTHCOMING ATTRACTIONS
MAY DATES

		Members	Guests
Fri. (17)	CHRIS FARLOWE WITH PURPLE DREAM	7/6	10/-
Sat. (18)	ALAN ELSDON JAZZ BAND	7/6	10/-
Sun. (19)	BOB MILLER AND THE MILLERMEN	7/6	10/-
Mon. (20)	**BILL HALEY AND THE COMETS** with the SHIRALEE	10/-	12/6
Wed. (22)	THE DELROY WILLIAMS SHOW	5/-	7/6
Thurs. (23)	THE SHIRALEE	5/-	7/6
Fri. (24)	**JAMES AND BOBBY PURIFY** with the GRENADES	7/6	10/-
Sat. (25)	THE MOJOS WITH THE SWEET RAIN	7/6	10/-
Sun. (26)	KENNY BALL JAZZ BAND	7/6	10/-
Wed. (29)	THE COMPLETE HERBALIST	5/-	7/6
Thurs. (30)	EDWIN STARR with the Evolution	7/6	10/-
Fri. (31)	CHICKEN SHACK with the Grenades	7/6	10/-

JUNE DATES

Sat. (1)	THE ROCK 'N' ROLL REVIVAL SHOW with MR. MO's MESSENGERS	10/-	12/6
Sun. (2)	THE PYRAMIDS	7/6	10/-
Wed. (5)	JETHRO TULL with the Epics	5/-	7/6
Thurs. (6)	FIRESTONES	5/-	7/6
Fri. (7)	THE COLOURED RAISINS with the Light Brigade	7/6	10/-
Sat. (8)	**HERBIE GOINS AND THE NIGHT TIMERS** and the SHIRALEE	10/-	12/6
Sun. (9)	**THE HONEYBUS** ("I can't let Maggie go") with the Delroy Williams Show	10/-	12/6
Wed. (12)	MR. MO's MESSENGERS	5/-	7/6
Thurs. (13)	THE SHIRALEE	5/-	7/6
Fri. (14)	AYNSLEY DUNBAR RETALIATION with the Light Brigade	7/6	10/-
Sat. (15)	**THE FASCINATIONS, ALSO GOMEZ COOPER AND HIS INCREDIBLE CHICAGO GANGSTERS**	10/-	12/6
Sun. (16)	THE PYRAMIDS	7/6	10/-
Wed. (19)	MR. MO's MESSENGERS	5/-	7/6
Thurs. (20)	THE FIRESTONES	5/-	7/6
Fri. (21)	SPENCER'S WASHBOARD KING with the Complete Herbalist	7/6	10/-
Sat. (22)	LAMB BROTHERS SHOW with the Shiralee	7/6	10/-
Sun. (23)	NOEL AND THE FIREBALLS	5/-	7/6
Wed. (26)	SAVOY BROWN BLUES BAND with the Light Brigade	5/-	7/6
Thurs. (27)	THE SHIRALEE	5/-	7/6

SPECIAL WEEKEND ATTRACTION

Fri. (28)	AMBOY DUKES with GEORGE PAUL JEFFERSON	7/6	10/-
Sat. (29)	**THE BONZO DOG DOO DAH BAND** with the Complete Herbalist	10/-	12/6
Sun. (30)	THE FREDDY MACK SHOW	7/6	10/-
	Tickets are available in advance at a reduced rate for all three nights	20/-	25/-

WOW! We really did 'Rock Around The Clock' that night. Everyone thoroughly enjoyed that

evening of authentic old fashioned Rock'n'Roll. And all that genuine rock'n'roll music for ten bob – 50p.

"See you later alligator
In a while crocodile"

"Get into that kitchen
and rattle those pots and pans"

"Well - it's one, two three o'clock…four o'clock rock
We're gonna rock around the clock tonight….."

Bill Hayley and his Comets were Rockin' that joint in Beckenham that night. The Shiralee were in excellent support.

I only wish I could have met my hero Elvis. Okay, okay he got a bit overweight, but I think I could have looked Elvis straight in the eyes with no awkward visual side defects.

I started to expand College Entertainments. I advertised for a PA who would co-ordinate all the college PR work. But instead of getting a cold, calculating female robot I employed a woman who was passionate and had that feminine magic called 'IT'. The gorgeous Mary Margaret Kelly was that girl and we became best friends. Then one magical day I realised I was madly in love with my best mate. She became the LOVE of my life.

She had answered an advert in The Stage newspaper which she never usually bought. Fate took a hand that day. It contained my show biz job ad. I interviewed ten talented female candidates for that job of 'College Co-ordinator'.

Mary shone like a diamond compared with the others. Mary was always a very special person. We all miss her so very much.

Would she know my name?
Would she feel the same?
Would she help me stand?
Would she hold my hand?
When we meet again…in heaven

I bloody well hope so.
I loved that woman so very much…
We shared THIRTY HAPPY YEARS together.
I miss her like mad.

I was as excited at being near her when she was 57 as I was dating her when she was 27, her age when we met. That's some marriage.

She was tough and feminine, strong and fair, resilient and highly talented. I always loved being in her company. We wrote ten books together and had five children. But not necessarily in that order. Mary, my darling, you are forever a primary source of inspiration and you are deeply missed by us all.

Whenever I think of the buzz of the Sixties my heart skips a beat. I can still feel the vibes generated by the vigor and energy of those times. After the boring, 'stagnant pond' 1950's life was worth living again. I wish you could share those Sixties experiences. Just for one more time. The sheer thrill of excitement generated during that special decade. That era of The Beatles, The Rolling Stones, Pink Floyd, Led Zeppelin, The Who, David Bowie and so many more.

This revisit to the sixties is not me being some precious old hippie wearing rose coloured retro glasses. It was a life and generation changing decade. I'd love to show you all those splendid attractions and music events I attended throughout the thriving 1960's.

Oh My Kingdom for a Tardis!

#TRACK 1
-HARD ROCK - HOT SEX-

PINK FLOYD

F*ck! F*ck! F*ck!
They were not available.
F*ck!
Was it because it was for the Queen –The Monarchy?
F*ck!
I was lost in confusion.
F*ck!
I was in complete panic and in deepest of deep shit!
F*ck!
My business was on the line.

I had to do much much better.

I could not get Pink Floyd for the Royal Charter Ball to be held in the presence of Her Majesty Queen Elizabeth and the Duke of Edinburgh.

The Royal Charter in 1967 gave the Royal College of Art, based in Kensington Gore, independent university status with the ability to award its own degrees. Consequently the R C A's students' social committee asked me to book Pink Floyd to top the bill at their Royal Ball. As I said, an event to be celebrated in the presence of royalty.

A well-known group had to be booked to headline this musical extravaganza. The RCA social committee trusted me to book Pink Floyd. They thought it was a guaranteed booking and I knew it was not.

Disaster beckoned.

Pink Floyd had played for me many times at the RCA Students Union gigs. They were the resident group. They were very popular with all those flamboyant art students. In those days, Pink Floyd featured a unique light show at all their performances. Among the RCA audience was David Hockney, considered now to be our most influential British artist.
I naively thought that I only had to mention

the R C A and Her Majesty and Pink Floyd would come running and instantly grab the booking. How wrong I was. Their office said they were unavailable - and that was that.

The Students Union felt let down and criticized me. They blamed me personally, 'You should have made a provisional booking many months before…' It was termed 'penciled in'. 'You should have booked Pink Floyd the minute you heard about our exceptional royal event…' The Student's Union committee and their Social Secretary were furious with me.
They felt that I had failed them.

My judgment was on the line because I *assumed* Pink Floyd would accept the royal gig. I could easily lose my lucrative rolling contract with the RCA, worth many thousands of pounds to my company – College Ents.

Pink Floyd were the most successful group to emerge from the underground scene. They had hitherto played gigs at the Marquee and the Roundhouse. They also performed regularly at the UFO club, the club that promoted the flourishing hippy theme. Pink Floyd eventually moved on and Soft Machine became the resident group. The UFO club had a serious run in with West End police. The boys in blue eventually forced it to close down.

Pink Floyd also appeared regularly at Middle Earth. DJ Jeff Dexter usually hosted nights in this Covent Garden club. Groups that played there, in addition to Pink Floyd, were The Who, The Bonzo Dog Doo Dah Band, Fairport Convention, Soft Machine and *Tyrannosaurus Rex* with Marc Bolan. All these groups/bands eventually worked for me in various venues and colleges across the land.

After signing to new management, Peter Jenner & Andrew King, the group secured a contract with EMI. The first single was Syd Barrett's 'Arnold Layne'. About a transvestite who steals underwear off the clothes lines. This track reached number 20 in the UK charts. The follow up single 'See Emily Play' reached number 6.

Their first Album was entitled 'The Piper at The Gates of Dawn'. Many tracks on the LP featured compositions by Syd Barrett. His authority in Pink Floyd waned after he fell under the heavy influence of hallucinogenic drugs.

I had tried like mad to get the Pink Floyd group for the royal gig because, among other things, their rock stock was rising fast. The Social Secretary begged me to sign them for the ball. Their line up did not change until early 1968 when the highly talented but unpredictable Syd Barrett was replaced. I am privileged to have booked the original Pink Floyd for the Royal College of Art. They were the super nova of rock groups. They were always very special.

Syd eventually 'retired' to be near his family in Cambridge. After many years of living in the rock music wilderness he took up gardening as a favourite past time. Syd sadly passed away in July 2006.

The original line up was:

Syd Barrett – Vocals, guitar;
Richard Wright - Keyboards;
Roger Walters - Bass;
Nick Mason- Drums

I had to find a suitable replacement as a headline act. Word spread like wild fire on the college circuit that I had fucked up and let The RCA down by not securing Pink Floyd for Her Majesty. If I didn't acquire an excellent comparable act then my name would be mud and my business badly tarnished.

I could be dead in the water in no time. Other colleges would change allegiance.

There were many new agents on the scene from the mid-sixties onwards. I was the 'old man' on the scene at the ripe old age of twenty five.

It was a crazy, quick tempo frenetic business. You had to keep ahead of the game. You both lived on your wits and willed yourself to win or you died in the process. Just left to wither on the vine of failure…

Throughout the 1960's and early 1970's I was Managing Director of several fast expanding entertainment agencies. However, it took many years of blood, sweat and many tears before I made the breakthrough into the big time.

Life was hard but the exhilaration of that frenetic period kept me going. There was a magical buzz all around. That quintessential period started on 1 January 1960. Stardust was scattered all over us 'Sixties Kids'. The 50's were tedious. That decade should have been deleted from history, except for Elvis, Chuck Berry and Little Richard.

And if it wasn't for Producer Jack Good ('Oh Boy' ITV rock show - circa 1958) then that period would have been as dull as dishwater.

I remember walking down Carnaby Street, Soho, London in the late 1950's, all the shops were boarded up. Business was dead. No growth, no hope. Just brainless restraint on potential talent.

Then suddenly it was like somebody had switched a bright light on. The sun came out - the sky was blue. Our time had come, and it was cherished by us all. New businesses sprang up, young people with many new ideas.

Some just talked the talk but most walked the walk. It was all happening all over London and would spread throughout the nation. New music, new designs and new fashions. And add fresh sparkling ideas. Innovation had arrived with a stylish flourish.

People clever enough to spot the trends became the next generation of the nouvous riche, no matter what their educational or family backgrounds. It became a young egalitarian society. I was an orphan boy from Brixton who mixed with kids from Harrow and Eton. We were all in it together, we were equals.

Just like Mike D'abo publishing a song with me. The song is still on my catalogue, registered with PRS. It's called 'When I Think Of You'. If it had been 'Glad rags' I'd be writing this on a yacht. It was a fast moving and thrilling music scene, where everyone was either in a group or managed one.

I had made an audacious start. I was only 19 and had to learn about being an agent pretty damn quick. My first office was dingy and a tad smelly. The Soho sewer had no respect for anyone, especially a teenage rock music agent.

The editor of The New Musical Express once ventured into my office to say 'Hello'. He quickly departed after sniffing the air. My small office was on the third floor at 7, Archer Street, Piccadilly, London. W.1. No postcodes in those days.

There was no natural light through my office window. It glimpsed out onto a grim and grubby panorama of decaying back walls. They were a part of a cluster of crumbling Victorian buildings housing brothels, gaming clubs, clip joints and strip tease parlours. I looked out onto an assortment of Soho rooftops, with their lopsided chimney tops, leading to a network of rotting and broken fire escapes. This scene depicted the authentic Soho in the early 1960s.

However, behind those crumbling walls lay a Soho that was rampant. Not only was Soho a seedy, sinful area but it was also an exciting place with a beating heart of joyous love for life and sexual adventures.

Thankfully, the weekly office rent was only £2.10s (Two pounds and fifty pence). An amount I could just about afford. My landlord, the well-known Soho hairdresser Sid Siger, occupied the ground floor shop. Access to my small third floor office was via the shop's side passage.

The sweet smell of the hair oils, circa 1960, lingered in the air. There was a certain sexual nuance about those evocative smells. I then ran up the rickety, twisting staircase to my office. Westminster Council later condemned the building. My main agency phone number was GERrard 4000. The dial on the phone had a combination of letters and numbers.

✯ ✯ ✯ **Society Entertainments**
STAR ATTRACTIONS INTERNATIONAL

SUPPLYING ALL THAT IS BEST IN ENTERTAINMENT

ORCHESTRAS - CABARET - HAWAIIAN - STEEL DANCE BANDS -
FOLK - JAZZ GROUPS - HIT PARADE ARTISTES - DISCOTHEQUES

6a/7 ARCHER STREET, LONDON, W.1

Telephones: GERrard 4000
REGent 8555/6/7

It would now be 0207 437 4000. I am never tempted to ring that number, in case I answered it - in some kind of quantum leap time warp. 'Four thousand, can I help you?'

However, I did once try to obtain the number GERrard 4001 from Post Office Telephones. No chance, it was the number of a local brothel. In those days, the Post Office owned the telephone system. BT was to come later during Thatcher's innovative period in office. All exchanges were quaintly named after their districts.

Therefore, you had such dialing code names starting, LORds, PRImrose Hill, FINchley, MORnington Crescent and BRIxton. When I lived on the estate my number was TULse Hill 8855, the number being 885 8855. Dialing codes for London came in later.

Mornington Crescent has many connotations with a BBC Radio Four programme called, "Sorry, I Haven't a Clue" which Humphrey Lyttleton chaired until his death. Humphrey was a renowned jazz musician. He charted in the 1950s with his famous instrumental "Bad Penny Blues".

The sound engineer who mixed and co-produced on that session was later to become my boss. He was the legendary Joe Meek. He produced 'Telstar'. The first instrumental million bestseller.

A play and a film have been produced, called 'Telstar', to depict Joe's much troubled life. He was always a great guy with me. He once took me into his quiet room and conducted a séance with Buddy Holly. Very spooky!

Because he was gay some might put another interpretation on it. No way, Hose. I was deeply into women. And anyway Joe was in love with his handsome Russian waiter.

I shared the third floor, at number 7 Archer Street, with a sheet music typesetter. They still set the music and lyrics in metal letterpress in the early to mid-sixties. Later, technology put that company out of business.

That little typesetting company was wiped off the face of the earth. The lesson? Progress or die.
After the music typesetter business went to the wall, a pleasant, softly spoken, Jewish tailor moved in. It was quaint seeing him stitching, cross-legged on the

cutter's bench. I remember listening to Celtic winning the European cup in 1967.

We all crammed into the 'sweatshop' and listened to his crackling transistor radio. That was a good day for British football, or should I say Scottish football. My two Scottish grandsons, who live near Glasgow, would want me to say the latter.

Soho and the West End of London were very different in those days. Life and times were along established indigenous lines, not as diverse as they are today. I could walk down Gerrard Street (now China Town) and not see a single soul. Unbelievable but true.

Although I did once bump into a secretary from the Rik Gunnel Agency, based in Gerrard Street. She was very excited and called over the road to me. "Hello Peter, today is the release date of Georgie Fame's first L.P. We're celebrating." *How many years ago was that?*

Archer Street, Piccadilly has always held a certain fascination for me. I was once working in my small third floor office, on a hot summer's day, when I heard someone shouting loudly from the street. I went down to investigate and see what all the fuss was about. Cassius Clay (Mohammed

Ali) had arrived there for a press photo session. Cassius was making jokes with the press and TV crews.

He was publicising his fight with Henry Cooper at Wembley. I thought he was a man mountain. The back of my neck is still a little stiff from looking up at him. Although our Henry knocked Cassius down, in that fight, Cassius survived. He went on to become a world champion and global hero. Both Cassius and I were aged 21 years of age on that sunny June day back in 1963.

At about that time, I also remember the popular comedian Marty Feldman looking for work as a drummer. This was years before he found fame as a TV and film star. He looked a little pathetic and most vulnerable, like a frail Jewish orphan in the wind.

The orchestra and band 'fixers' arrived every Monday afternoon. Archer Street was crowded with musicians seeking gigs and residencies. I remember Marty, looking out shyly from the back of the crowd. His distinctive heavy lidded eyes fluttering and darting from side to side. Marty was looking in all directions for that important gig from a friendly 'fixer'. A gig meant hot food and 'a cuppa char' – A cup of tea.

My other vivid recollection was coloured red. Blood red. A young guy had been stabbed in the chest and was bleeding profusely. He was slumped on the doorstep of Sid Siger's hairdresser's shop. Sid was taking the dreadful incident in his stride. However, he was rather reluctant to have his pure white hairdressing towels used to staunch the flow of blood. A policeman wandered into view. He was young, weedy and pasty faced; he almost passed out when he saw the bloody scene. I think the victim survived, not so sure about the young pallid faced copper.

When I first started as an agent there was almost nothing doing. I had nowhere to go, no one to see. I knew no one in the music business. Everything was really quiet, the phone never rang. I was apprehensive about my rock music agency surviving. I was also between girl friends at this point in time, I felt sad, lonely and forlorn. To kill the time and the loneliness I sometimes played Barbra Streisand's first ever LP. Barbra was my saviour. Thank you for making feel less lonely, you beautiful Jewish princess.

I smiled at "Come to the Supermarket in Old Peking" and felt emotional when listening to "A Sleepin' Bee" and "Cry Me a River". I was depressed and contemplated giving up the business but suddenly decided to stay and fight.

First, I got off my ass and went to see every live music venue in Soho. I then advertised for groups, mixing and matching from there. The business grew but only very slowly. For several years I just scraped by and the dreaded telephone bills increasingly sent me to the edge of insolvency. As I mentioned my big break came when I started booking the colleges. It all happened with a call from Brunel University. That was my turning point to future success. That college gig showed me the way to the future. They paid well and the cheques were guaranteed. Everything snow balled from there. So, dear reader, NEVER give up.

I love being a sextet. I am still in my sixties as I write this chapter today. How old will I be when I finish it? I've so much to share. I am as old as Beatle Paul Mc. We are both sixty plus and very much enjoy female company. And getting lost in desire and passion.

I was always short of money. Bills were a constant problem. I never received any capital to start my business. Chris Wright got his family to capitalise him generously when he started the globally successful

Chrysalis. I was as poor as a church mouse when I saw that small lineage advertisement in the London Evening News. The office was available in Piccadilly for £2.10s per week. I could just pay that rent if I got a job. I walked to Leicester Square and was interviewed for a job as an usher at the JC cartoon cinema, on the corner of Leicester Place. It is now a restaurant. I got the cinema job and was paid £10 - ten pounds per 40 hour week.
I was happy because my music agency was now being subsidised. It might survive.

All I had to do was to become a 'Loony Toons' hustler. Part of my cinema duties was to shout at the Leicester Square crowds, 'Roll up...Roll up...Road Runner, Daffy Duck and Bugs Bunny all for half a crown.' A half a crown was 2s.6d - Just twelve and half pence.

Another bonus were the beautiful usherettes. We shared some great times. But I had to wangle the circumstances so that the girls would become more readily available to me. I was devious, cunning and very naughty. When promoted to Chief of Staff I only employed young gays as ushers. That way I had no competition. All's fair in love and usherettes.

When my agency got too busy to cope, I quit the cinema job. I had nightmares about giving it up. I was in turmoil about losing this subsidy. There were always the telephone, advertising and travel costs to pay for. And the cost of the occasional Castella cigar to favoured social secretaries.

I need not have worried about that extra income from the cinema. My business strategy was beginning to pay off and my business grew. So I moved next door to first floor offices at 6A Archer Street. My new office was near the Lyric pub and opposite The Orchestral Association. It was almost next door to the famous Windmill theatre. Many a comedian started his career there, including Peter Sellers. The striking illuminated display at the front of theatre was a pair of woman's legs immortalised with the legend, 'We Never Closed'.

My 'modern' new offices had an en suite bathroom.
Only pleasant smells in this new office set up. Next to my own office was a large open plan office. It is here that I employed several bookers. Most were former Social Secretaries from high spending universities.

The reception was spacious and was occupied by many a pretty secretary over the years. One day a sparkling vivacious Scots lass became employed as my College Co-ordinator. We co-ordinated so well that we shared over thirty happy years together. We also produced shows, music and a best-selling book, 'The Children That Time Forgot'. That book has been reprinted five times in the UK and Ireland.
It was also published in the USA, Canada, Japan, France, Holland, Hungary and Czechoslovakia. It is now successful as an Amazon book and also on Kindle. However, our best joint productions are our five fabulous children. Mary Margaret was a joy to live and work with.

My new Archer Street landlords were the Lyric theatre group headed by Sir Lew Grade. The last encounter I had with him was when I was a runner at Associated-Rediffusion, TV House in Kingsway. I later became ITV's first ever trainee. I mixed with all the early ITV stars, Hughie Green, Michael Miles and a young David Frost in the Features department as a researcher working for programme head, Caryl Doncaster.

Many years later I was an associate producer {with Mary} on a David Frost programme called 'Night Visitors' and

David Frost hosted. The programme was produced on location in Cardiff Castle.

Back at AR-TV the famous studio 9 was in the basement of TV House. I remember seeing colleague John Reardon starting his TV cameraman career in that studio. John went on to become a renowned TV director/producer at London Weekend Television.

On another occasion I went down to studio 9 to watch Ted Heath and his Orchestra rehearsing for a broadcast. Years later Ted Heath (with his orchestra) played his very last performance at the annual GLC dinner and dance.

The event was arranged by my agency. I negotiated the gig directly with Ted, he gave me a full ten per cent. Many of the big names split commission, in which case I would only receive five per cent. Pop music programme 'Ready, Steady Go' was later broadcast from studio 9 in the basement of TV House.

I always used Lew's ATV (Associated-Television) lift because it took me to the sixth floor without stopping. Remember, I was a sixteen-year-old teenager in a very great hurry. But on this occasion I was in too much of a hurry. I had a run in with the

Russian bear. I found him in the lift glaring at me eyeball to eyeball. As he blew cigar smoke in my face he told me to 'Fuck Off'. He personally knew all his runners and decided I was not one of them. Lew detested AR-TV and all who sailed in her.

However, these new offices were good. Light, airy with a positive feel. The rent paid to Lew's theatre company was also reasonable. I ran four companies from my new Archer Street offices. In addition to *College Entertainments Ltd*, there were other general booking agencies, *Star Attractions International, Society Entertainments. I also formed Artistes International specifically to represent the fast emerging ethnic actors.* I got work for these actors at ITV and West End theatre.

I employed a black booking manager, Ronald Swire, who had many contacts in the business. He was also a personal friend of Lionel Bart, the celebrated composer who wrote several hit musicals including *Oliver. Ronnie told me that Lionel Bart's toilet was a 'throne made of gold'.* Bling!

My motivation to form Artistes International? I was sick of seeing white British actors wearing 'gravy powder'. This was on the false assumption that ethnic actors could not play the necessary parts. This was not only true in TV drama, but also TV comedies like 'It Aint 'Alf Hot Mum'.

Some people thought that the casting of the white actor Michael Bates, as the Indian bearer Rangi Ram, to be an example of blackface. However, the show's producers had been very averse to the idea of casting a white actor to play one of the Indian characters. They said that they were forced to relent owing to the lack of high-profile Indian actors available at the time.

Not true.

There were several highly talented ethnic actors around who could have played that part, including Saeed Jaffrey and Renu Setna. Both on my books at Artistes International.

The clubs I booked, via Star Attractions, in Soho included:
St.Moritz (still there at 161 Wardour Street.)
Les Enfants Terrible
La Discotheque
St Germaine
Sam Widges
Whisky A Go Go
Last Chance Saloon

The King Creole - formerly Cy Laurie club

And at the Notre Dame de France, 5 Leicester Place, London we promoted lunch time discos. 'We' being me and a musician who became world famous, it was Roger David Glover. He was a member of Episode Six at the time. Sometimes we made a profit, sometimes not.

Over the years many more universities put their trust in College Entertainments Ltd. However, the contract I had with the Royal College of Art was the best deal I'd had with any university up to that time.

I later bought a house near Streatham Common with the increasing proceeds of my newfound 'College Ents' profits.

Previously I had struggled for years living off the commissions from 'Ten Pound Groups' that I booked in those Soho clubs and coffee bars. The ten per cent commission being a solitary one pound note. But it was College Ents that changed everything for the better. If I had given up in the wilderness years then I would never have experienced that sweet smell of success.

There were so many bookings coming in from colleges and universities, increasing month on month, I could hardly cope. In 1968 I was just too busy and nearly had a breakdown. My new baby daughter 'V' saved me. I only had to look into her big beautiful eyes and it brought peace, sanity and tranquility.

However, back at the RCA, trying to discover a group to replace Pink Floyd was proving a nightmare. I could not find a comparable group to fill this headline spot. I spent many panicky hours on the phone trying to put this musical event together. I could not afford to have it snatched away from me by another agent. That would be a disaster for my business. And I could not let Her Majesty or the RCA down.

However, it was difficult to find a group that would satisfy the Students Union and time was running out. They were on the brink of giving this massive musical event to another agent to book and produce. If that happened then word would spread that I had screwed up – Big time!

Hallelujah! My guardian angel appeared and rescued me at the very last minute.com. Rod Stewart suddenly became available fronting The Steampacket with Long John Baldry featuring Elton John and Julie Driscoll. They were readily accepted by the committee. Yippee!! I had already booked Rod on a number of previous occasions. He had worked for me when he was featured with Jimmy Powell and the Dimensions.

Later Rod worked with a small rock'n'blues combo. They played in many of the London beat clubs around London. I was involved in a Tuesday night residency for him in Wardour Street, Soho.

Rod was second vocalist in John Baldry's 'Hoochie Coochie Men' who played for College Ents at many Unis'. I was blessed with this booking because Steampacket were eventually recognized as the first ever UK super group.

The line up was:
Long John Baldry - Vocals
Rod Stewart - vocals
Julie Driscoll - vocals
Reg Dwight / Elton John - Piano
Brian Auger - Organ
Vic Briggs - guitar
Richard Brown - bass guitar
Micky Waller - drums

What an incredible blend of voices and instruments.
BALDRY + ROD + JULIE = Rock vocals made in

Rock music heaven! The atmosphere that night was electric with breathless anticipation. In addition to all those famous faces in the Steampacket I had an assortment of other spectacular musical talent performing that night.

I had seen dozens of groups over the years but The Steampacket were the crème de la crème. They rocked the roof off the Royal College of Art and students were dancing in the street. Everyone agreed that Steampacket were a tremendous success. So much so that the committee fell back in love with me again. I only wish YOU could have witnessed that unique rock music sound. It blasted everyone away; students, lecturers and, not least, the royals. That combination of fantastic rock musicians will linger with me forever more. Just fabulous! Sadly, that incredible sound was never replicated because the various musicians were signed to different labels.

Soon after the band split and many of those artistes drifted on their own journeys to super stardom, in most cases.

The Steampacket would have stopped the TV show LATE with Jules Holland in its tracks. If fate had ever allowed such synchronicity to have occurred. As it turned out, Steampacket were more appropriate for that royal occasion than Pink Floyd would ever have been. Pink Floyd were more suited for the student residency gig. And they continued playing their weekly gigs at the college.

This Royal event was an extravaganza and a celebration of exciting rock and soul music. The occasion cried out for a group that put on a proper professional performance. Not a precious foursome that emanated out of the underground scene. I had succeeded with my show stopping top of the bill act. As a postscript, I would like to send a note of thanks to Rod et al for saving my business with their performance.

In addition to Steampacket, I had booked a variety of musical entertainers. These included The Graham Bond Organization. Graham's group with rock legends Jack Bruce and Ginger Baker. I also booked a trad jazz band. They were lively fun. There was also a West Indian steel band with low flying limbo dancers. And to further brighten the evening with some colourful flare I featured fire-eaters and belly dancers to wobble the night away.

To complete the musical set I booked an outrageous Manchester folk group, Faz 'n' Roger. This duo could have been arrested for 'injury' to a royal person.

David Twigg had written a centre page article for the London Evening News about them. They had released, on Fontana/Philips records, a folksy song entitled "Happy Poor Man Blues".

The music newspaper of the time, The Disc, tipped it for the 'Hit Parade'. The chap responsible for signing them at Fontana was Jack Baverstock. He was an enormous help and arranged to put some strings on the recording. At no extra charge to me. Faz n Roger were fierce anti monarchists. One of the lads turned to me and said that they had decided to 'gob' on Her Majesty.

I am an ardent British republican but even the thought of spitting at Queen Elizabeth was too much. At the end of the day, it was the institution I rebelled against not the royal person. The royals had been born into it, they had to get on with it. They were products of fate, their lives confined to a virtual gold fish bowl.

Those two teenage republican tearaways came close to having me locked up in the Tower of London. Behind my back, they conspired to get into the gallery and 'gob' on the Queen's dress from above.

Unbeknown to Her Majesty and her security team they did just that and I was angry.

Elizabeth had devoted her life to this country with selfless dedication. But on this occasion she went back to the palace with a large dollop of 'Manchester phlegm' on her gown. I never forgave that folk duo for that disgusting behaviour. I sacked them. But I still think the UK should be a republic.

Don't give me the argument that it will affect tourism. The Republic of France always get far more visitors than the UK. I am a dedicated post Elizabethan republican. Charles will be a disaster. I understand he wants to become the next King George, Keeping it warm for his grandson George Cambridge.

My objections include the fact that there are too many hangers on. Taxpayers meet the cost of many royal events, including Prince Andrew going golfing via helicopter rides.
The royal hierarchical system creates an unequal society. While they maintain the centre of power, we will remain a society of social grading. We arrive in this world with nothing and depart with nothing. We must become a more egalitarian society. The

way to achieve this is to retire the royals to their country estates. They will join the big society and attend endless charity events. The sooner the better.

Faz 'n' Roger were made to realize that they had transgressed. Gone over the line of decency. The folk group departed London and returned to Wythensaw, Manchester.

Back in 1967 Elizabeth was almost forty. She was smiling and enjoying my musical presentation. As Her Majesty swayed to the music, her large handbag was seen to be swinging in rhythm with Rod's melodious musical performance. On that day in June 1967 I was concerned about her security. There did not seem to be any.

I had arrived in the early afternoon to supervise and produce that evening's events. I was however surprised that there were no royal detectives checking the venue out. I am certain that if this event had taken place a couple of years later the RCA would be crawling with the royal protection officers. However, the lack of any royal protection concerned me. Another British cock up. The IRA did not become actively dangerous until Prime Minister Callaghan, son of a Catholic waitress, put the troops into Northern

Ireland. He did it for the best of reasons, to protect the Catholic population. The very people who eventually turned against the British army.

I will never forgive the IRA for blowing to pieces a very special lady. She was Gerry Edgeson's wife who was murdered in a Mayfair restaurant. Gerry was sitting next to her and survived, such is the way of bomb blast. It kills some and leaves others to grieve.
Gerry was my financial backer - also known as a theatrical angel - for one of the musical shows I produced.

I personally checked out all the roadies and hangers on taking part in the various set ups. But there was not a single protection officer around. One visitor we had to that royal gig was a pro film stunt man. I still do not know why he was there. He was definitely not an undercover royal cop. Perhaps a disappointed Pink Floyd fan? He spent the entire time slagging off film director Michael Winner. Telling me that Michael was a nutcase expecting stuntmen to perform death defying scenes. All in the cause of reality in film.

The Queen's consort, Philip, was in attendance. He was sharing his views with a group of female awe struck art students.

They muttered and giggled subserviently, as if metaphorically touching their forelock. Philip beamed with pleasure. With David Hockney in the audience I should have booked an attractive well hung nude male dancer, just wearing white socks and no jock strap.

I must tell you about a tenuous link with Rod Stewart and a sexy lass from the other side of the Penines. Whisper, whisper! This is true confession time. A couple of years before the royal RCA musical celebration I made love to a Rod Stewart groupie on the floor of my office. She was a beautiful girl from Lancashire. She had come down from Manchester because she was nuts about Rod Stewart. A hot Rod groupie. He obviously wasn't interested so I got her on the bounce. This girl was so full of hot sex that I was getting just too excited.

The smell of her cheap decadent perfume. Her hot breath. Our French kissing getting me thoroughly overheated. Her grabbing my hand and forcing it onto her hot stiffening nipples. She expertly knew how to stiffen a boy up. Maximum - fully extended. And how to get a guy to a point of no return.
I was in that auspicious position. But I was incapable of holding back. If she had said

NO at that point I would have exploded. Do women realise the power they have over us boys? I bet they do!
As I took her underclothes off I noticed a peculiar smell. I thought about it a few days later and went to see my doctor. We were in the middle of the swinging sixties, everyone was crazy and I had to take care. I didn't want anything to interfere with my exciting love life. I took all precautions so that I could stay fresh, stay clean for a special relationship.

I was sent to a VD clinic where they gave me a thorough examination. This included slicking a long cold metal instrument up my back passage. As the young male doctor performed this painful task, he asked, "Did you engage in any homosexual activity?"

Although I had many gay friends, colleagues, and associates I never had even the slightest urge to indulge. As one of my characters, in my play 'The Dispossessed', says ... 'I don't have a homo erotic muscle in my body.'

"No!" I hastily replied, "I love women, always have."

I was given the medical all clear. The doctor wanted to know where he could contact the girl so that she would not spread the disease. I had no idea, I never saw her again. She had left the office in the early hours and caught a taxi to the station. She said she was going straight back to Manchester. She only came down to see Rod Stewart at his London gig.

In spite of that appalling smell, she was very good 'in the hay', or should that be 'on the office floor'. After our vigorous love making session she turned to me, while still lying on the floor, and said those words that are pure magic to any man…"You're good Peter, I really enjoyed it!"

I hope she eventually got medical treatment. Venereal Disease can be a handful. I was thankful that I was clean.

A couple of years later I started a close relationship with a nineteen-year-old nurse. A lovely blonde girl with a pleasant personality. She eventually became my first wife, and mother to my beautiful and loyal daughter 'V'. She is now happily married and lives in the north. She has given me two wonderful grandsons.

I have another whisper to tell you about. My captivating young wife, whatever her other faults, had excellent judgment. One night she proved it by cuddling up to me in bed and whispering… "Darling, you have the most perfect manhood."

Hard Rock ~ Hot Sex.

Yes indeed!

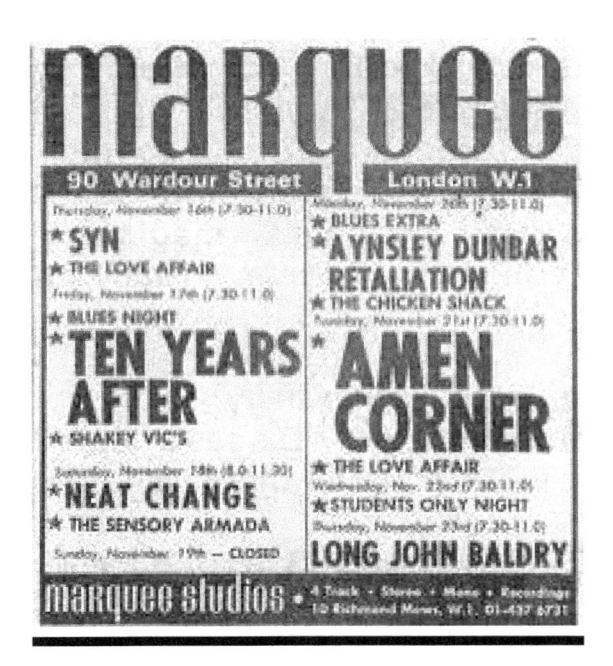

#TRACK 2
-THE DECADE OF THE MILLENNIUM-

The decade of the millennium started on Friday 1st January 1960. That day heralded a new era of innovation, ground breaking technology and an explosion of British rock groups. Those Rock Gods grew in popularity throughout that decade, and then took over the global music scene, especially in America. The U.S. dominated the music industry prior to the 1960's and I resented it.

As an angry anti U.S young teenager, in the late '50's, I would go up to the record counter in Woolworth's in Brixton, like a young punk rocker, and 'scowl and spit' at the U.S. stars. Guy Mitchell, Doris Day, Frank Sinatra, Bing Crosby etc.

It was the decade that spawned a new generation of ambitious young people who craved the smell of success and, equally, instant notoriety. Some were ruthless in their pursuit of fame and fortune, others fell into the arms of the law.

Two of my song writing friends went to prison for smoking marijuana in the early '60's. They did six and five years each. The second guy, Freddie, only did five because the judge also went to Eton. Unbeknown to me they smoked it in my Archer Street office. When I tell this story people cannot believe that you were sent to prison for smoking marijuana.

You also went to prison if you were actively gay until Parliamentary reform in 1967. And prior to 1861 you were hanged for homosexual activity in Great Britain and its Dominions.

In the USA January 1960 saw the start of the series of famous Johnny Cash concerts behind bars.

In 1962 the Beatles first single release, 'Love Me Do / PS I Love You', went to number 17 in the UK and to number 1 in the USA.

The Beatles first record *almost became their last*.
Many do not realize or appreciate that the world came very close to annihilation.
The Cuba nuclear missile crisis had the potential of ending all life on earth as we know it. I still relive that chilling experience. It was back in October 1962, I was 20.

I heard recently, on BBC Radio 4, that some parents, at the height of the crisis, woke their children up to say 'goodbye'. One of the children, now an adult and parent, said that it was a fantastic feeling to experience the sun rise that following morning.

I can see myself walking down Charing X Road towards Trafalgar Square. All of us feared an imminent nuclear attack. London would become an inferno causing 'my eyes to melt down my cheeks'.

I admit that I was petrified as I continued my onward journey to Trafalgar Square. We were expecting an instant attack. Would I make it to Nelson's column?

Away from the dramatic headlines a little known drama was being played out in a Russian nuclear submarine. In that sub was the hero to humanity, Arkhipov. Russian Naval Commander Vasili Arkhipov. He was second in command of Soviet Foxtrot-class B59. This diesel powered nuclear submarine was trapped under the sea by several U.S. Navy destroyers and the aircraft carrier USS Randolph.

None of the officers or crew of the B-59 knew if war had broken out. The captain, Valentin Savitsky, and the political officer, Ivan Maslennikov, wanted to launch a nuclear tipped torpedo.
It is this single incident that could have sparked the launch of WW111. The war to end the world.

In the event Arkhipov argued with his highly emotional colleagues and persuaded them not to fire. The submarine began to surface, not least because the batteries were low and the air conditioning failed. In spite of being amongst its pursuers, the B-59 eventually sailed home.

As I have survived that potential nuclear holocaust please allow me to walk you through my favourite decade…The Nineteen Sixties.

1960

The Beatles started out in 1960 as The Quarry Men. Then they became The Beatals before becoming The Silver Beetles.

In May of that year they auditioned to back one of my favourite singers, Billy Fury. However they ended up backing Johnny Gentle, touring in Scotland.

On that tour they temporarily changed their names: 'Long John Lennon', 'Paul Ramon', 'Carl Harrison' and Stuart Sutcliffe became Stu de Stael. Later in the year The Beatles made their first public performance at the Kaiserkeller in Hamburg.

The Beatles record together for the first time. They include bassist Walter Eymond, of Rory

Storm and the Hurricanes, at the Akustic Studio, Hamburg.

George is deported for being under age for night club work after midnight.

Towards the end of 1960 Paul McCartney and Pete Best are arrested for alleged arson in Hamburg. They were accused of setting fire to their living quarters at the Bambi cinema and thrown into jail.

On their return to Liverpool The Beatles perform at the Litherland Town Hall. This was the start of Beatle mania.

* * * * *

In Germany Elvis was made a sergeant in the US army. He was discharged soon afterwards and continued his recording career.

➢ I can remember drinking with friends and discussing his first post army record release. I couldn't decide about 'It's Now or Never' at first but I soon got to like it. It topped the charts on both sides of the Atlantic. His follow up was 'Are You Lonesome Tonight'. Elvis couldn't reach some of the notes and had to 'drop in' many times to complete the recording.

➢ Elvis' first recording company was Sun Records. I visited Graceland and Sun's studios recently. Amazing experience.

- I am a big fan of this Super Nova and could feel his spirit in both venues. I 'sang' into Elvis' own Sun Studio microphone, circa 1955.

On the music scene Dick Clarke's famous music show, Bandstand starts.

The Everly brothers release 'Cathy's Clown'.

Chubby Checker creates a new dance craze called 'The Twist'.

The comic pop song 'Itsy Bitsy Teenie Weenie Yellow Polkadot Bikini' goes to number 1.

1960 also witnessed the first ever gig by Jimi Hendrix.

* * * * *

Senator John Kennedy announces his candidacy for the US Presidency.

- My father told me at the time that Kennedy did not stand a chance. Dad said that many people thought that Catholics had two heads. I became a Catholic when I married Mary.

Senate passes the Civil Rights bill. 'Lady Chatterley's Lover' was ruled 'Not Obscene' in the U.S courts.

Various nuclear tests are carried out, mostly by France.

There is a serious race riot in Jacksonville, Florida and the first oral contraceptive comes onto the market.

USSR create their own space oddity, two dogs into space.

Widower Vernon Presley, Elvis' dad, weds Dee Alliot.

➢ *I, on the other hand, felt sad and lonely during this dark period. Roy Orbison's 'Only the Lonely' always resonates with me, reminding me of that lonely period. I remember sitting alone in an Indian restaurant in Soho's Lisle Street.*

➢ *How different things are now with my large loving family.*

Alfred Hitchcock's 'Psycho' opens in NYC.

➢ *I saw it at the A B C in Brixton. My friend, Alan Jacobs, and I thought the film was excellent, especially the horrific shower scene. Thrilling.*

After winning the Olympic light heavyweight

gold medal Cassius Clay goes on to win against Tunney Hunsaker in the autumn of 1960.

➢ I met Cassius Clay (Muhammad Ali) in Archer Street, Soho when we were both 21 in 1963.

Ricky Valance is number 1 with 'Tell Laura I Love Her'.

I was involved with the cover version by John Leyton.
John's producer was Joe Meek, I was his assistant.
One of my all-time favourite songs is 'Spanish Harlem' by Ben E King. That track became a big hit in 1960 as did his other excellent recording, 'Stand By Me'.
Another great favourite was Ray Charles. I once played 'What I'd Say' so loudly and persistently that I almost got arrested.

Ray's great big hit at this time was the memorable, 'Georgia on My Mind'.

1961

In February The Beatles performed at The Cavern for the first time. But it was for the lunchtime session. In March they were promoted to the evening session. Later that month they travelled to Germany and appeared at the Top Ten club on the Reeperbahn.

In November The Beatles' future manager, Brian Epstein, visited the Cavern Club.

Brian managed his family's record department in North End Music Stores (NEMS), and heard many teenagers talk about the group. Brian visited the Cavern to see what all the fuss was about. His visit was the start of a phenomenal change in the global music business. It would never ever be the same again. The Beatles were to go on and break the stranglehold that the US mafia had on the music industry. The U S of A had always ruled the music airwaves.

On the anniversary of my birthday, December 9th, The Beatles played their first gig down south in Aldershot. Only 18 people turned up, it was not advertised properly.

Four days after that disastrous gig Mike Smith, Decca Records A&R manager, visited Liverpool to see The Beatles play at the Cavern club.

*****

The seeds of nuclear conflict are sown on 5th January '61 when the U.S. breaks relations with Cuba. The missile U.S. Minuteman ICBM is tested.

In N Y C the New Yorkers were freezing. On Feb 3 they had the largest snowfall registering 44.2 CM.

In London the black taxi drivers were angry again. Mini cabs were introduced for the first time.

➢ The majority of Taxi drivers were Arsenal supporters. Over a forty year period I only met one guy who supported Chelsea.

➢ When I was a poor kid cycling around the streets of London the rudest, aggressive and meanest drivers were Black Cab Drivers.

➢ They were dangerous, not only because they detested cyclists but most of all they hated us kids on bicycles.

➢ They missed hitting me or running me over many times. Maybe I had that Chelsea habit of nutmegging them.

There's hope for me yet. On March 13th 79 year old Pablo Picasso married his model girlfriend. She was 37 year old Jacqueline Rocque.

In April Yuri Alexeyevich Gagarin became the first person to orbit the earth in Vostok 1.

JFK gives the fateful go ahead for 1,400

Cuban exiles to attack Cuba in the Bay of Pigs fiasco. The attempt to overthrow Castro ended disastrously. This failed attempt to terminate this staunch ally of the USSR was JFK's darkest hour.

In May Alan Shepherd becomes the first American to go into space on board Freedom 7.

My one time cricket hero, Freddie Truman, takes 5 wickets for no runs in 24 balls to rip through the dreaded Aussies. Best sports highlight in this year of 1961.

And in Israel they welcomed their one millionth immigrant.

In August the UK applies to become a member of the European Common Market. Why bother?

In Germany, that same month, the construction of the Berlin Wall begins. There is an outbreak of nuclear 'cock waving' between the two world enemies. The USSR resumes exploding atomic bombs and JFK orders the USA to start underground nuclear bomb testing. The USSR nuclear tests are at Novaya Zemlya. JFK advises his fellow Americans to start building nuclear bomb shelters.

In November JFK sends 18000 'military advisors' to Vietnam.

On a lighter note Sean Connery, the former Edinburgh Co-op milkman, is named as the first ever James Bond.

As the Beach Boys perform for the first time JFK flies to Bermuda to meet Harold McMillan. Was he a Beach Boys fan?

1962

In January The Beatles travel to London to audition for Mike Smith and Dick Rowe at Decca records. They recorded fifteen tracks.

Soon after they signed a management contract with Brian Epstein, Dick Rowe rejected them. A costly and embarrassing mistake for which he paid for forever more.

In March The Beatles make their first radio broadcast for the BBC in Manchester. They perform at the Playhouse theatre in a programme called 'Teenager's Turn (Here We Go)'. The following month Stuart Sutcliffe dies of a brain hemorrhage aged 21.

In June The Beatles record for the first time at Abbey Road studios. Ringo Starr replaces Pete Best on drums. In October Parlophone Records / EMI release 'Love Me Do' / 'PS I

Love You'.

The Beatles appeared on Granada TV in a programme called, 'People And Places'. In November and December they travel to Germany again and appear in the Star Club Hamburg.

*****

The Stones start Rolling together.
Their creator and original instigator was a large Scots boy called Ian Stewart.

Mick and 'Keef' move into a flat in Edith Grove, Chelsea. They have no money, no food and hardly any shillings to stuff into the meter to keep the freezing winter at bay. But they had three female trainee teachers, living on the floor below, to keep them warm and lovingly occupied. But can you believe it? 'Keef' never fancied any of them. In July The Rolling Stones play their very first gig at The Marquee.

The Isley Brothers release their famous song, 'Twist and Shout'.

Island Records starts trading on the 4th July.

> *My wife Mary hated going to their offices. To go upstairs visitors had to climb a spiral staircase where all women's undergarments were exposed to the gaping male employees on the ground*

floor.

David Frost appears in satirical BBC TV show: 'That Was The Week That Was'.

Telstar. 1st geosynchronous communicator satellite, is launched. The satellite's name is later used as the title of the first instrumental million selling record. The producer was my mate Joe Meek.

➢ *My friend and ex-boss Joe Meek records his tune using The Tornadoes. There was a claim by a French composer that Joe had stolen the theme tune. It was finally resolved in Joe's favour, just days after his untimely death.*

The United States navy establishes the S.E.A.L.S for the first time. Generations later they shot that infamous terrorist dead in Pakistan.

Civil Rights leader Martin Luther King is jailed in Albany, Georgia. There was a large minority of white bigots who hated blacks, gays (in those days the term was *'queers'*) and rock'n'roll.

In August Jamaica gains independence of the UK after 300 years of British rule. Now they are thinking about giving up on our monarchy being involved at any level. Good luck to them. Monarchy should be banned after Elizabeth departs her mortal coil.

Shooting begins on Dr. No, the new Bond movie.
I have seen EVERY Bond film. 'Skyfall' is the best.

➢ *Skyfall is my favourite, nonstop action.*

Fidel must be feeling paranoid. Not only does Pope John excommunicate him but also JFK bans all trade with Cuba except for food and drugs. The blockade of Cuba begins.

John Glenn, first American to orbit the earth in Friendship 7.

The palace of the South Vietnamese president is bombed, and the very first US citizen is killed in conflict in that dreaded war.

1963

The Beatles are well ahead in the pop rock race.
Their second single 'Please Please Me' / 'Ask Me Why' was featured on TV in 'Thank Your Lucky Stars'. In February they tour with Helen Shapiro, who tops the bill. 'Please Please Me' tops the charts in both The New Musical Express and Disc but only makes

number 2 in the BBC charts.

* * * * *

➢ This was my breakthrough year. I started booking a better class of venue. At the start I was booking coffee bars and Soho beat clubs.

➢ Some of the bands I booked during '63 included *The Tridents* (Jeff Beck), *The Roosters* (Eric Clapton), *Yardbirds* (Keith Relph / Top Topham / Chris Dreaja), *Casey Jones and the Engineers* (Eric Clapton / Tom McGuiness).

➢ *Manfred Mann* (Paul Jones, Manfred Mann, Mike Hug), *John Mayall's Bluesbreakers* (John Mayall / John McVie / Roger Dean), *Graham Bond Organisation* (Graham Bond, Jack Bruce, Ginger Baker, Dick Heckstall-Smith).

I also booked some folk singers. Their fees were so low it was hardly worth it, commission wise. But I never ever turned down a booking because I valued every single gig. Why? Because I came from the hard knocks school of Brixton where life taught you to fight every inch of the way. *Nobody gave you nuffin'.*

I'm pleased to report that the composer, Ralph McTell, of 'The Streets Of London' worked for me several times, and folk singer Billy Connolly, of The Humblebums, once.

As mentioned the year opened in freezing conditions. The coldest winter for a couple of hundred years.

The Rolling Stones got a hot break by getting the residency at Crawdaddy Club in Richmond.
Andrew Loog Oldham, ex PR man, saw them there and became their manager. Andrew got them a contract with Decca Records. He produced all their early and best songs.

Their first release, a cover of Chuck Berry's 'Come On'. The 'founding father' of the Rolling Stones, Ian Stewart, was told to take a back seat.
He looked 'too normal'. Andrew realised (correctly) that the Stones had to be bad boys against the lovable cuddly Fab Four.

The Rolling Stones original line up was: Mick Jagger, vocals; Keith Richard, guitar / vocals; Brian Jones, guitar / vocals; Bill Wyman, bass; Ian Stewart, piano; Charlie Watts, drums.

* * * * *

First disco opens in L A – The Whisky a Go Go

In the UK the Beecham report suggests many

railway lines and stations should be closed. An efficiency drive to save millions.

Russia boasts a 100 megaton nuclear bomb.

Winston Spencer Churchill becomes the first UK honorary citizen in the USA.

British Minister of War, John Profumo, resigns due to alleged affair with Christine Keeler.

JFK signs law allowing equal pay between the genders.

In Alabama Governor Wallace tries to prevent black students registering at University of America. But JFK says segregation is morally wrong and that it is 'time to act'. And three thousand black students boycott public school.

On a visit to Berlin JFK makes his famous speech, 'I Ich bin ein Berliner' – I am a Berliner.

Israeli Prime Minister David Ben-Gurion resigns and is replaced by Levi Eshkol.

In the UK thieves steal £2.6m in the great train robbery.

A church in Birmingham, Alabama is bombed

and several African-American small girls are killed.

British Premier Harold McMillan resigns and chinless wonder Alec Douglas-Home takes over. Winston made some disparaging remark about the new prime minister. 'Who is he?'

Dr.Who is first broadcast on 23rd November.

Six year old Donny Osmond debuts on the Andy Williams show.

JFK is assassinated in Dallas by Lee Harvey Oswald. Lyndon B. Johnson becomes the 36th US President. It is said that everyone knows where they were at the moment that Kennedy was killed.

➤ *I was walking across Shaftsbury Avenue towards my office in Archer Street, Soho. I felt a tap on my shoulder, it was local gangster Italian Tony. He was visibly upset as he told me, 'The Kennedy brothers have been hit and they're both dead.'*

On November 24th, live on TV, Jack Ruby fires at Kennedy's murderer Harvey Oswald and kills him, while police look on.

1964

The Beatles LP 'Meet the Beatles' is released in the USA. In the US Cashbox magazine 'I Want To Hold Your Hand' goes to number 1.

George changes the name of his publishing company to 'Harrisongs'.

➢ And without my permission, George!

➢ My music publishing company is called Peter Harrison Music.

The EP 'All My Loving' is released in the UK.

73 million viewers see the Fab Four on the Ed Sullivan Show. And they play two concerts at Carnegie Hall in New York.

A single 'Twist And Shout'/There's A place' is released in the US only. The mop tops start filming 'A Hard Day's Night'.

The Beatles collect the Show business Personalities of the Year award. I am invited to attend the press launch of John's first book, 'In His Own Write'. It sells out in no time.

The Beatles hold the top six positions in the singles charts in Sydney, Australia and the top five positions in America's Billboard chart.

John attends a literary lunch in his honour.

The Beatles are portrayed at Madame Tussaud's in Baker Street.

'A Hard Day's Night' has royal charity premier at The Pavilion, Piccadilly.

The lovable four play Kansas City Municipal Stadium on their day off – for $150,000.

* * * * *

Rolling Stones tour UK with 'The Ronettes'. Rod Stewart records 'Good Morning Little School Girl'.

Beach Boys release the iconic 'I get around', goes to Number 1.

Bob Dylan completes UK tour. He's booed in Dublin.

Jan & Dean record, 'Little Old Lady from Pasadena'.

EMI rejects 'High Numbers' (The Who).
* * * * *
Stanley Kubrick's 'Dr. Strangelove' premiers.

➢ *I saw this when it opened. Peter Sellers was brilliant.*

Cassius Clay, Muhammad Ali, beats Sonny

Liston in round 7.

➤ *Cassius (Muhammad) was always my favourite.*

First pirate radio starts in UK, 'Radio Caroline'.

➤ *Jack Good, 'Oh Boy' producer, suggested I join the radio pirates as a disc jockey. If I'd been a public school boarder I'd have been psychology prepared for the experience. I declined and instead became a young successful rock music agent in London's West End.*

Ian Smith becomes premier of Rhodesia.

➤ *My wife Mary, then in her early 20's, was determined to move there after securing a good job. I met her in 1971, thank God she ran into the following challenges because obviously we would never have met.*
Diplomatic tensions were at breaking point after Rhodesia flouted international law by claiming independence from the UK.
There was a zero tolerance policy towards emigration to Rhodesia. Harold Wilson's government tried to vehemently dissuade British Nationals from emigrating to Rhodesia.

➤ *Mary was officially warned about sailing to*

Africa.

As she was about to board the boat to Africa she experienced a life changing moment. Two government immigration officers told her that if she sailed they would lose her British passport. Her choice was to carry on with her journey, with a strong possibility of never seeing her family again, or returning to the bosom of her family. She chose mum and dad and forfeited her considerable boat fare.

She had worked day (In a travel agency) and night (In West End theatres) for over a year. It was solely to save the necessary amount of money to take her to a new life in Africa. She was shattered by the experience and very unhappy at the time.

➢ *Thank you Mary for changing your mind about moving to Africa. Your decision changed and formed many lives.*

Joe Orton's 'Entertaining Mr. Sloan' premiers in London.

➢ *I liked this emotionally painful and twisted play.*

Nelson Mandela is sentenced to life in prison in South Africa.

➢ *Mary's cousin from South Africa walked passed her embassy in Trafalgar Square and* was shocked by the intensity of protest.

Civil rights act passed in USA after 83 day filibuster.

➢ There was a bigoted white majority against this bill.

Turkey begins air attacks on Greek Cypriots in Cyprus.

➢ My Greek Cypriot accountant had land taken from him by the Turks. He was seething with hatred but could do nothing.

The TUC supported left wing 'Daily Herald' newspaper finally shuts its doors on its Fleet Street offices.

➢ Although my grandfather was a working class (prison officer) conservative he always read the Daily Herald, a labour party paper that was part owned by the T U C (Trades Union Congress).

TV pilot of 'Star Trek' being developed.

➢ My kids loved the series.

Also 'Dr.Zhivago' in production.

➢ I really did enjoy this classic.

US comedian, Lenny Bruce, is convicted of obscenity.

➢ *I could feel the angst and raw anger from this man
   at the performance I attended.*

1965

The Beatles 'Eight Days A Week' is released in U.S.

The Beatles fly to the Bahamas to start filming 'Help'.

'Ticket to Ride' is released in April.

Beatles awarded the MBE.

➢ *There is a strong rumor that the cuddly mop heads smoked hash in Buck House toilets. Oh my dear, whatever next?*

A new LP released in the USA, 'Beatles V1'.

John publishes his second book, 'A Spaniard in the Works'.

'Help!' had its premier at the London Pavilion.

Record audience of 55,600 in the Shea Stadium NYC.

Elvis meets The Beatles at his home in Beverly Hills.

The single 'We Can Work It Out' is released. The LP 'Rubber Soul' & 'Help' is released in UK.

ITV broadcasts 'The Music of Lennon & McCartney.'

* * * * *

Rolling Stones release, 'The Last Time', (I Can't Get No) Satisfaction', and 'Get Off My Cloud'. They are fined £5 each for urinating in the street,

Rod Stewart joins The Steampacket with Brian Auger, Julie Driscoll and Reginald Dwight (Elton John). THANK YOU ALL for saving my business in 1967 at the Royal event at Royal College of Art.

The Who release successful singles, 'I Cant Explain', 'Anyway Anyhow, Anywhere' and 'My Generation'.

Jeff Beck replaces Eric Clapton in the 'Yardbirds'.

* * * * *

On the 30th January State Funeral of W.S.Churchill.

Joe Orton's 'Loot' premiers in Brighton.

➢ *Appropriate location!*

Righteous Brothers release classic, 'You've Lost That Loving Feeling'. Goes to # 1.

Alabama state troopers clash with 600 black protesters in Selma.

Luther King leads 25,000 to protest in state capital Montgomery, Alabama.

US involvement in Vietnam increases, 1st combat troops go in. Australian troops also go in, but UK refuses.

➢ Harold Wilson is a brave man standing up to U S pressure.

Although I am a Conservative I rated socialist Harold Wilson highly. For his intellect, courage and good positive thinking.

Edward Heath replaces Alec Douglas-Hume as leader of the Conservative party.
➢ Heath was a poser and a weak man. Gave in to the unions and too attached to the EU.
➢ 'My Fair Lady' wins a host of awards.

Cigarette ads banned on UK TV.

Bob Dylan booed for playing electric guitar at concert in Forest Hills, New York.

➢ *I remember Bob Dylan got the same treatment in Dublin. They were used to big showbands. A skinny kid with a mouth organ and an acoustic guitar was like getting no value in Irish eyes.*

1966

Beatle George marries Patricia (Pattie) Ann Boyd.
Honeymoon in Barbados.

➢ *Long after that wedding George came to visit me at my office. Unannounced. I was in the middle of a complicated university booking. He could not wait. He left before I could say, 'We're both Harrisons'.*

A documentary was made called 'The Beatles at Shea Stadium' and broadcast on British TV.

➢ *Never Saw it. But I attended ITV's Wembley studio with The Beatles when they made a TV programme which Jack Good produced. It featured Lulu and Long John Baldry.*

Beatles release an EP, 'Yesterday'.

The Beatles last 'proper' UK concert is

performed at Empire Pool Wembley.

The Beatles single, 'Paperback Writer' / 'Rain' is released. This single was performed on 'Top of the Pops'. *I wonder who the DJ presenter was on that broadcast. Could it have been the alleged despot - J.S.?*
The Beatles tour Germany, Japan and the Philippines.

➢ Philippines - I remember the big trouble the mop heads landed in when they 'ignored' Imelda Marcos.
The Beatles EP 'Nowhere Man' is released in the UK.
London's Evening Standard publish an interview with John Lennon in which he states that The Beatles 'are more popular that Jesus.'

Brian Epstein later holds a press conference in New York to try and explain John's remarks.

➢ This remark caused The Beatles a lot of problems, especially with the US Christian Fundamentalists.

The Beatles fly to Chicago to commence their final tour of the U.S. John holds a press conference and apologises for his 'stoopid' remark about Jesus. As borne out in the next story about a 'Beatles bonfire'.

Beatles pelted with rotten fruit at Memphis concert.

Radio station KLUE in Longview, Texas organizes a public 'Beatles Bonfire'. But the next morning the radio station was wiped off the air when a lightning bolt destroyed the transmission tower.

The very last Beatles performance in America was on the 29th August at San Francisco's Candlestick Park.

The Beatles start recording 'Sgt Pepper'.

➢ When this was released I played it over and over again.

John meets Ono for the first time when he attends an art exhibition 'Unfinished Paintings & Objects' at the Indica Gallery in November 1966.

* * * * *

David Bowie releases first record, 'Can't Help Thinking About Me'.

➢ *David worked for me at The Lyceum. Great guy.*

Jack Good features The Kinks and The Who, last 'Shindig' show.

Famous Beatles' Liverpool club Cavern

closes.
Brian Jones' final performance as a 'Rolling Stone'.

Simon and Garfunkel's 'Sound of Silence' goes to number 1.

Buffalo Springfield form with Stephen Still and Neil Young.

Neal Diamond charts for the first time with 'Cherry Cherry'.

Dance theatre of Harlem opens.

Rolling Stones appear on the Ed Sullivan show.

'The Monkees' debut on NBC-TV.

➤ Inventive crazy storylines – catchy zany pop music.

Rolling Stones hit with 'Paint it Black'.

➤ *Great song by those superstar songwriters Mick and Keith.*

Jimi Hendrix Experience debut at 'Bag 'O Nails' club. He records 'Hey Joe' and writes Purple Haze' at the 'Upper Cut Club'.

➤ *Jimi played guitar with his teeth. Jimi's*

supreme.

* * * * *

NYC emergency as 400 die of heart failure and breathing problems.

Harold Wilson wins the general election in UK for Labour party.
➢ Harold was one of the shrewdest politicians, brilliant brain.

Child murderers Ian Brady and Myra Hindley put away for life.

The Severn Bridge in Bristol is opened.
President Lyndon Johnson urges Congress to enact gun control legislation.

➢ That was more than 50 years ago. How many more victims?

Race riot in Waukegan, Illinois, U S A.
US President LBJ signs Freedom of Information Act.

The drug LSD declared illegal in USA.

'Cabaret' opens in New York City.

1967

The Beatles sign a new nine year contract

with EMI.

The famous cover photo of Sgt. Pepper's Lonely Hearts Club Band album is shot by Michael Cooper.

Paul goes to the Bag o' Nails club to see Georgie Fame and meets Linda Eastman.

Brian Epstein holds a launch party of Sgt. Pepper at his home.

'A Day In The Life' banned by BBC, overt drug mentions.

Paul admits on TV that he has taken drugs.

The Beatles perform 'All You Need Is Love' for 400m viewers. John, Paul, George, Ringo and Brian Epstein sign a petition in favour of marijuana in The Times newspaper.

John, George and Paul meet Maharishi Maheshi Yogi at the Hilton hotel and become interested in transcendental meditation.

On the 27th August Brian Epstein found dead in bed at his London home. His funeral in Liverpool is a private family affair and The Beatles do not attend.

Paul calls a meeting about The Beatles future at his home in Cavendish Avenue, St Johns

Wood, London. A memorial service is held for Brian at the New London Synagogue in Abbey Road.

John and George attend a party heralding the opening of the Beatles' Apple Boutique.

Paul and Jane Asher announce their engagement.

The David Frost TV show features Paul defending the Magical Mystery tour.

The Beatles 'Penny Lane' goes to Number 1 John Lennon takes delivery of psychedelic Rolls Royce.

* * * * *

Turtles go to Number 1 with 'Happy Together'.

Pink Floyd release first single 'Arnold Layne'.

Elvis and Priscilla Beaulieu get married in Las Vegas.

Aretha Franklin goes a Number 1 with 'Respect'.

Pink Floyd's first U.S. tour

Ian Anderson and Glenn Cornick form 'Jethro Tull'.

* * * * *

Green Bay Packers beat Dallas Cowboys 34-27 NFL.

PBS-WABW TV Channel 14 begins broadcasting in Pelham, USA.

Louisville draft board refuses exemption for Mohammed Ali.

The Boston Strangler, Albert DeSalvo, sentenced to life in prison.

In Chicago there are 23 inches of snow and 50000 vehicles are abandoned.

Apollo 1 fire kills astronauts Grissom, White and Chaffe.

'Let's Sing Yiddish' closes after 107 performances in NYC.

US troops start largest offensive of Vietnam War.

➢ Harold Wilson again refuses to send British forces to Vietnam.

Some Australians went. That war provoked more protests than any other event in the 1960's.

Stalin's daughter, Svetlana, asks for political

asylum in the USA.

JFK's body is moved, temporary grave to a permanent memorial.

Abortion legalized in Colorado.

Mohammed Ali is stripped of his boxing titles. And sentenced to five years in prison for refusing induction into the US army.

Maureen Witon runs female world record marathon: 3:15:22.

'Sing Israel Sing' closes after 14 performances at Brooks Atkinson Theatre NYC.

Six day war between Israel and Arab countries. Israel occupy Gaza. Israel wins war and much territory.

Queen Elizabeth Hall opens on the South Bank, London.

1968
My wonderful daughter, Virginia Ann, is born in Tooting, London. We were worried because she was a 'breech' birth. To me my lovely daughter 'V' was always bigger than The Beatles. She's a superstar.

Pattie Harrison features in an Ossie Clark

fashion show in London which John and George attend.

The single 'Lady Madonna' is released.

John and Paul fly to NYC to set up their Apple business venture.

John and Yoko appear in public for the first time. They attend a launch party and Press conference for another Apple Boutique.

The National Theatre's production based on John's book, 'In His Own Write', opens at the Old Vic in London.

The Beatles 'Yellow Submarine' has its world premiere at the London Pavilion. Piccadilly, London.

Jane Asher announces that her relationship with Paul is over.

Ringo quits the Beatles during the recording of the 'White Album'.
He later rejoins the group.

John and Yoko are charged with possession of cannabis and obstructing the police. And John & Yoko appear inside a bag at Royal Albert Hall.

John and Cynthia are divorced.

John Lennon art exhibition is called, 'You are here'.

Beatles Magical Mystery Tour at number 1 for 8 weeks

* * * * *

David Gilmour joins Pink Floyd.

Mick Jagger and Marianne Faithful arrested at drugs bust.

Rolling Stones release 'Jumpin' Jack Flash'.

Simon and Garfunkel go to number 1 with 'Mrs. Robinson'.

Rock group 'Yardbirds' disband.

Crosby, Stills and Nash debut.

➢ C S N -They became massive – both here and there.

Bobby Goldsboro hits with 'Honey'.

Elvis gets Gold for 'How Great Thou Art'.

Johnny Cash and June Carter wed.

Otis Reading posthumously receives gold record for 'Dock of the Bay'.

➢   *Go to YOUTUBE now and get a listen to this iconic track.*

* * * * *

Dr. Christian Barnard carries out heart transplant.

Leo Fender sells Fender guitars for $13 Million.

In the US postage stamps rise from 5c to 6c.
'The Prime of Miss Jean Brodie' opens in NYC.
Additional 10,500 US soldiers go to Vietnam.

One of the most controversial battles begins in Vietnam – Battle of Khe Sanh.

'Rowan and Martin's Laugh In' debuts on NBC.

Former VP Richard Nixon announces candidacy for President.

Former President Dwight Eisenhower shoots a hole in one. Ike used to spend more time on the golf course than in the White House.

For first time BBC broadcast news in colour.

➢   Makes no difference, the news is still more black than white.

Temperamental senior Labour cabinet minister, Gordon Brown, has a fall out with Premier Harold Wilson. Fat, drunken and useless George resigns.

➢ *I bet there was a big sigh of relief at the Foreign Office when Brown resigned. He was a buffoon.*

➢ *Some Labour cabinet ministers did not have a clue. Many ran to Harold with every little problem. They all put pressure on Wilson, it eventually leads to his premature death. H.W. was a brilliant politician; many of his ministers were duffers.*

General Motors produces its 100 millionth automobile, The Oldsmobile Tornado.

➢ *I just love those big flash gas guzzlers.*

Martin Luther King is assassinated in Memphis, Tennessee.

British Conservative politician Enoch Powell delivers his controversial 'river of blood' speech, about immigrants.

➢ *Edward Heath sacks Powell from the shadow cabinet.*

'Half a Sixpence' opens at Broadway Theatre

NYC for 512 performances.

Mary Bell, aged 11, strangles a four year old.

➤ Such a tragedy.

'Hair' opens at the Biltmore Theatre for 1750 performances.

➤ I, with my new teenage bride, went to see original 'Hair' in theatre in Shaftsbury Avenue. We both enjoyed the show. Sensational nudity. Cocks had never had such a rude display.

Student riots in Paris – Over 1000 injured

Senator Robert Kennedy is shot dead.

➤ It was sickening. Live on TV. Where were his minders?

Garfield Sobers hits six sixes in one over.

➤ I don't like cricket, I love it.

1969

The Beatles begin filming 'Get Back', which is eventually retitled 'Let It Be'.

George walks out on the 'mops' but is persuaded to return.

Paul confirms officially that he is not dead. There were rumors because he walked across the Abbey Road zebra crossing in bare feet. And in some places in the world bare feet means…
In their last filmed performance The Beatles record 'The Long and Winding Road'.

Alan Klein becomes The Beatles' business manager.
Although Paul refused to sign contact, it is alleged.

Paul and Linda attend the launch of Mary Hopkins debut album, 'Postcard'.

Ringo begins filming 'The Magic Christian'.

Paul marries Linda Louise Eastman at Marylebone Registry Office, London.

George and Pattie are busted for cannabis possession.

John marries Yoko Ono abroad.

Paul refuses to sign a contract appointing Allen Klein's company ABKCO. Company that publishes most of the Stones catalogue.

The single 'the Ballad of John and Yoko' is released in the UK. John, Yoko and 'friends' record 'Give Peace A chance'.

John, Yoko, Kyoko and Julian are involved in a bad car crash north of the border.

John Lennon's 'Two Virgins' album declared pornographic in New Jersey, USA.

All four Beatles are photographed walking across the zebra crossing in Abbey Road for the cover of 'Abbey Road'. The recording of this album is the last time they record together.

The Beatles are photographed for the last time at Yoko's home.

Sgt. Pepper album in charts for 88 weeks.

➢ *I loved that album so much that I wore it out.*

Beatles say 'bye. They appear on the roof of their Apple H.Q.

John returns his MBE to the Queen.

➢ *Well done John. BUT why take it in the first place?*

John quits The Beatles. You wonderful, talented scousers.

* * * * *

Jethro Tull's debut album, 'This Was'.

Cream release last album, 'Goodbye'.

Jimi Hendrix and Pete Townshend wage …'…battle of guitars.'

Jim Morrison exposes himself in concert. Gets arrested.

Brian Jones leaves The Rolling Stones. Mick Taylor replaces him

David Bowie releases 'Space Oddity'.

> *I just love that record. Love it!*

~THE SHIRALEE ~
- A GREAT 60's GROUP -

Left to right - Back row:
Graham Barnes - Lead Guitar/Vocals
Ken Golding – Vocalist: Mick Nolan - Drummer
Front row: - Case Cummings - Rhythm Guitar & Vocals
Bernie Clarke - Bass Guitar & Songwriter

#TRACK 3
-The Groups-

Throughout the 1960's and early 1970's I booked countless famous rock groups, some became legends. I also booked dozens of support bands, artistes and groups. One of the most popular groups on the circuit were The Shiralee. I produced their Fontana record.

They performed the A side, "I Will Stay By Your Side", live on BBC radio. And the B side, "Penny Wren", was played on the popular "Two Way Family Favourites". This programme was broadcast at lunchtime on Sundays and the audience was huge.

Over that period three bands that I booked were Number 1 in the charts at the time of their performance for me. I had booked them far in advance, for minimal fees, prior to their records scoring top spot in the music charts. All three acts honoured my original contracts, and never increased their fees.

1: Herman's Hermit's with *'I'm Into Something Good'*.

2: Honeycombs with *'Have I the Right.'*

3: Neil Reid with *'Mother of Mine.'*

Not everyone played the rock music game with the same honest endeavour. Sadly, some managers double-crossed me. I would phone and make a provisional booking only to find that they then contacted the social secretary and did the deal.

Thankfully it was a rare occurrence. If it had been rife in the business then it would have been curtains for me. I operated on a basis of good will. I could not afford to hold a grudge. I could phone that same manager a couple of days later and book this same group for another gig with no problems whatsoever.

Although I did have a row with impresario Robert Stigwood. He put his assistant on. I shouted, 'I don't want to talk to the oil rag, put the engine driver on.' I then spoke to Mr Choo Choo.

Here are some of the artistes, bands and groups I booked from 1960 through to 1972.

Some became legends...

AMEN CORNER
Amen Corner were Number 1 in the charts when I booked them for my one and only Rock Festival in Essex.

Can you believe that they were a bigger name than The Who during that period?
My children have never heard of them. I asked several people recently if they remembered the group. I usually got a blank stare with the words, 'Amen what?'

Back then Amen Corner would not take second billing to The Who. The Who would definitely not take second billing to Amen Corner. We almost did not have a festival. Artiste billing has been a headache for producers since those Greek tragedies way back when.

I still managed to get them both on the same bill. I designed the poster so that it appeared that they both got top billing.
Amen Corner where bottom left and The Who top right with a diagonal line [bottom right to top left] separating the names. That poster worked for both groups. Phew!

The band was named after The Amen Corner, a weekly disc spin at the Victoria Ballroom (later to become The Scene Club) in Cardiff, Wales, where every Sunday night Dr. Rock would play the best soul music from the United States.
Neil Jones (guitar) —Allan Jones (saxophone) —Blue Weaver (keyboards) — Mike Smith (tenor saxophone) Clive Taylor

(bass) — Dennis Bryon (drums). Initially they specialised in a blues and jazz-oriented style, but were steered by their record labels into more commercial pastures.

Their first singles and album appeared on Decca's subsidiary label, Deram but they left at the end of 1968 to join Immediate Records.
They were rewarded with a No. 1, "(If Paradise Is) Half as Nice" in early 1969, followed by another Top 5 entry, "Hello Susie". The final studio album was *Farewell to the Real Magnificent Seven*, with a cover version of The Beatles' "Get Back" released as their swansong, they disbanded at the end of 1969.

BRIAN AUGER

It was Brian who blended the 'Steampacket' music at the Royal College of Art Royal charter ball in 1967.
Brian, born 18 July 1939.

Brian incorporated jazz, early British pop, R&B, soul music and rock, and he has been nominated for a Grammy.
In 1965 Auger formed the group *The Steampacket.* His line up included Rod Stewart, Long John Baldry and Julie Driscoll. As I said before, this band was the best rock'n' blues outfit in the land.

They were proudly the first ever U K supergroup. Especially as Elton John was sometimes in the line up playing piano. Brian is a jazz and rock keyboardist, who has specialized in playing the Hammond organ. Auger has played or toured with artists such as Rod Stewart, Tony Williams, Jimi Hendrix, Sonny Boy Williamson

With Driscoll and the band, Trinity, he went on to record several hit singles, notably a cover version of David Ackles' "Road to Cairo" and Bob Dylan's "This Wheel's on Fire".

In 1969 Auger, Driscoll and Trinity appeared performing in the United States on the nationally telecast "33⅓ Revolutions per Monkee".

In 1970 he formed Brian Auger's Oblivion Express, shortly after abandoning the abortive "Wassenaar Arrangement" jazz-fusion commune in a small suburb of The Hague. The Oblivion Express served to cultivate several musicians.

Including the future Average White Band drummers Robbie McIntosh and Steve Ferrone, as well as guitarist Jim Mullen. Likewise, in 1971 he produced and appeared on Mogul Thrash's only album.

Two members of that band, Roger Ball and Malcolm Duncan, would also go on to form the Average White Band.

THE ANIMALS

The Animals were an English music group of the 1960s formed in Newcastle upon Tyne , they later relocated to London. Eric Burdon (vocals) - Alan Price (keyboards) - Chas Chandler (bass) - Hilton Valentine (guitar) - John Steel (drums)

They were dubbed "animals" because of their wild stage act and the name stuck. The Animals moderate success in their hometown and a connection with Yardbirds manager Giorgio Gomelsky motivated them to move to London in 1964.

They performed fiery versions of the staple rhythm and blues repertoire, covering songs by Jimmy Reed, John Lee Hooker, Nina Simone, and others.

Signed to EMI's Columbia label, a rocking version of the standard "Baby Let Me Follow You Down" (retitled "Baby Let Me Take You Home") was their first single.

The Animals were known for their gritty, bluesy sound and deep-voiced frontman Eric Burdon, as exemplified by their number one signature song "The House of the Rising Sun" as well as by hits such as "We Gotta Get Out of This Place", "It's My Life", and "Don't Let Me Be Misunderstood".

They were known in the U.S. as part of the British Invasion. The Animals underwent numerous personnel changes in the mid-1960s and suffered from poor business management.
Under the name Eric Burdon and the Animals, they moved to California and achieved commercial success as a psychedelic rock band, before disbanding at the end of the decade.

Altogether, the group had ten Top Twenty hits in both the UK Singles Chart and the U.S. *Billboard* Hot 100. The original lineup had a brief comeback in 1977 and 1983. There have been several partial regroupings of the original era members since then under various names. The Animals were inducted into the Rock and Roll Hall of Fame in 1994.

GINGER BAKER

Peter Edward "Ginger" Baker, born 19 August 1939 Lewisham, South London, is an English drummer, best known for his work with Cream and Blind Faith.

He is also known for his numerous associations with World music, mainly the use of African influences.

He has also had other collaborations with Gary Moore, Hawkwind and Public Image Ltd. Baker's drumming attracted attention for its flamboyance, showmanship and his use of two bass drums instead of the conventional single bass *kick* drum (following a similar set-up used by Louie Bellson during his days with Duke Ellington). Although a firmly established rock drummer and praised as "Rock's first superstar drummer", he prefers being called a jazz drummer. Baker's influence has extended to drummers of both genres, including Billy Cobham, Peter Criss, Bill Ward, Ian Paice, Nick Mason, and John Bonham. AllMusic has described him as *"the most influential percussionist of the 1960s"* and stated that *"virtually every drummer of every heavy metal band that has followed since that time has sought to emulate some aspect of Baker's playing."* Baker gained fame as a member of the Graham Bond Organisation.

And then as a member of the rock band Cream from 1966 until they disbanded in 1968.

He later joined the group Blind Faith.

In 1970 Baker formed, toured and recorded with fusion rock group Ginger Baker's Air

Force.
Baker formed and recorded with *Ginger Baker's Energy* and was involved in collaborations with Bill Laswell, jazz bassist Charlie Haden, jazz guitarist Bill Frisell, and pioneering afro beat musician Fela Kuti. He was also member of Hawkwind, Atomic Rooster and Public Image Ltd.

In 1994 he formed *The Ginger Baker Trio* and joined the bassist known as *Goo* Chris Goss.

KENNY BALL

I booked Kenny Ball and his jazz band many times over the years. His band's performances were always highly rated. But invariably I'd get a call, the morning after the gig, from someone in the support beat group.

"Kenny Ball said we are the best group he has ever played with. He said he is going to speak to his manager about making us…The next BEATLES!"

Kenny Ball , born 22 May 1930 Ilford, Essex, is an English jazz musician, best known as the lead trumpet player in Kenny Ball and his Jazzmen.

Ball began his career as a semi-professional sideman in bands, whilst also working as a salesman and for an advertising agency. He played the trumpet in bands led by Charlie Galbraith, Sid Phillips, Eric Delaney and Terry Lightfoot before forming his own trad jazz band in 1958. His Dixieland band was at the forefront of the early 1960s UK jazz revival. In 1961 their recording of Cole Porter's 'Samantha' became a hit, and in March 1962, Kenny Ball and His Jazzmen reached both #2 on the U.S. Billboard Hot 100 chart, and the UK Singles Chart, with "Midnight in Moscow".

The record sold over one million copies, earning gold disc status. Further hits ensued, including a version of 'March of the Siamese Children' from 'The King and I', which topped the pop music magazine, *New Musical Express* chart in March that year, and such was their popularity in the UK that Ball was featured, alongside Cliff Richard, Brenda Lee, Joe Brown, Craig Douglas and Frank Ifield, on the cover of the New Musical Express in July 1962, although in the U.S. they remained a 'one-hit wonder'.

In January 1963, New Musical Express reported that the biggest trad jazz event to be staged in Britain had taken place at Alexandra Palace. The event included George Melly, Diz Disley, Bilk, Barber, Alex Welsh, Ken Colyer, Monty Sunshine, Bob Wallis, Bruce Turner, Mick Mulligan and

Ball.

Ball became the first British jazzman to become an honorary citizen of New Orleans and appeared in the 1963 film, *Live It Up!*, featuring Gene Vincent.

CLIFF BENNET

Cliff's voice just blew me away. What a sound - what a blast. Cliff certainly had a unique forceful vocal delivery. Cliff Bennett and the Rebel Rousers were a 1960s British rhythm and blues and soul group.

They had two Top 10 hits with "One Way Love" (Charted 9 1964) and "Got to Get You into My Life" (Charted 6 1966).

Members include:
Clifford Bennett, vocals ;
Dave Peacock, lead guitar ;
Chas Hodges, keyboards, bass ;
Mick Burt, drums and Nicky Hopkins, piano.

In 1957 Bennett put together the first version of the Rebel Rousers.
They were good enough to attract the attention of record producer Joe Meek, with whom they recorded several singles that were leased to Parlophone. Bennett continued recording for Parlophone, including cover versions of "You've Really

Got a Hold on Me" and "Got My Mojo Working", but failed to make any impact.

They were signed by Brian Epstein to a management contract in September 1964 and their seventh release, "One Way Love" b/w "Slow Down", finally charted soon after. Their next, "I'll Take You Home" b/w "Do You Love Him", only got to #42 but "Three Rooms With Running Water" (written by Jimmy Radcliffe and Bob Halley) did somewhat better.

Then, in early 1966, while an opening act on The Beatles' last European tour, Paul McCartney played "Got to Get You into My Life" for Bennett.

The song would appear on the *Revolver* album later that year and was not to be released as a single so, with Paul McCartney producing the session, a #6 hit ensued, with Bennett's song "Baby Each Day" appearing on the B-side.

ACKER BILK

I once got a call from a promoter saying that he will book Acker again because he was so much fun. He had danced on the tables at the gig the night before.

Bernard Stanley "Acker" Bilk MBE, born 28

January 1929, is an English clarinetist. He is known for his trademark goatee, bowler hat, striped waistcoat and his breathy, vibrato-rich, lower-register clarinet style. Bilk earned the nickname Acker from the Somerset slang for 'friend' or 'mate'. His parents tried to teach him the piano but it restricted his love of outdoor activities including football. He lost two front teeth and half a finger in a school fight.

Bilk has claimed it affected his eventual clarinet style. He learned the clarinet while serving in the Royal Engineers in the Suez Canal after his friend gave him a clarinet that he had bought at a bazaar. By the mid-1950s he was playing professionally.
Bilk was part of the boom in traditional jazz in the late 1950s. He first joined Ken Colyer's band in 1954, and then formed his own ensemble, The Paramount Jazz Band, in 1956. Four years later, their single "Summer Set," a pun on their home county co-written by Bilk and pianist Dave Collett, reached number five in the British charts and began a run of eleven top 50 hit singles.

Bilk was not an international star until an experiment with a string ensemble and a composition of his own as its keynote piece made him one in 1962. He wrote "Stranger on the Shore" for a British television serial series and recorded it as the title track of a

new album in which his signature deep, quivering clarinet was backed by the Leon Young String Chorale.
The single was not only a big hit in the United Kingdom, where it stayed on the charts for 55 weeks, gaining a second wind after Bilk was the subject of the TV show This Is Your Life. As a result, Bilk was the first British artist to have a number one position on the *Billboard* Hot 100 singles chart.

"Stranger on the Shore" sold over one million copies, and was awarded a gold disc.

BONZO DOG DOO DAH BAND

I booked The Bonzos on many occasions. Mostly on the college circuit. I also booked them into The Mistrale Club in Beckenham and had a serious run in with Viv Stanshell. There was trouble! Viv had been drinking at the bar instead of going on for the second spot. The owner, Mike Loveday, asked me to hurry everything up, they were running late. Viv turned on me. He put his finger over his top lip and started doing goose steps up and down the bar. He was mimicking Hitler and saying that was me.
I refused to let him continue drinking and ordered him to go back on stage. He soon returned to the stage after I'd had a few firm

words in his 'shell like' (ear).

Watch The Bonzos on YouTube performing, 'Intro Outro'. The Bonzo Dog Doo-Dah Band (also known as The Bonzo Dog Band) were created by a group of British art-school wizards of the 1960s. Combining elements of music hall, trad jazz, psychedelic rock, and avant-garde art, the Bonzos appeared on an ITV comedy show, Do Not Adjust Your *Set. The director was my mentor, Adrian Cooper. What a lovely guy.*

Unusually for a band, the actual date of conception for the Bonzos is known: 25 September 1962. It was on that day that Vivian Stanshall (tuba, but later lead vocals along with other wind instruments) and fellow art student Rodney Slater (saxophone) bonded over a transatlantic broadcast of a boxing match.
Rodney Slater had previously been playing in a trad jazz band at college with Chris Jennings (trombone) and Tom Parkinson (sousaphone). Roger Wilkes (trumpet) was the founder of the original band at the Royal College of Art, along with Trevor Brown (banjo). They slowly turned their style from more orthodox music towards the sound of The Alberts and The Temperance Seven. Vivian was their next recruit , he and Rodney christened the band, The Bonzo

Dog Dada Band. *Bonzo the dog* was a popular British cartoon character created by artist George Studdy in the 1920s.

MARC BOLAN / T Rex

I booked Marc as a solo performer for the Mistral club, Beckenham. While I was talking to Marc I got a profound sense of loneliness and a touch of sadness. Whether I was picking up vibrations for his current state or for the future tragedy.
I will never know. Marc Bolan, born Mark Feld 30 September 1947. Died 16 September 1977. He was an English singer-songwriter, guitarist and poet.
He is best known as the founder, frontman, lead singer & guitarist for T. Rex, but also a successful solo artist. His music, as well as his highly original sense of style and extraordinary stage presence, helped create the glam rock era which made him one of the most recognisable stars in Britain.

Bolan grew up in post-war Hackney, northeast London, the son of Phyllis Winifred (née Atkins) and Simeon Feld, a lorry driver. His father was of Polish-Russian Jewish descent. Later moving to Wimbledon, southwest London, he fell in love with the rock and roll of Gene Vincent, Eddie Cochran, Arthur Crudup and Chuck Berry and became a mod, hanging around coffee bars such as the 2 I's in Soho. At the age of nine, Bolan was given his first guitar and began a skiffle band. While at school, he played guitar in "Susie and the Hoops," a trio whose vocalist was a 12-year old Helen Shapiro. At 15, he left school "by mutual consent".

Marc shortened the group's name to T. Rex and wrote and recorded "Ride a White Swan", dominated by a rolling, hand clapping back-beat, Bolan's electric guitar and Finn's percussion.

Bolan died on 16 September 1977, two weeks before his 30th birthday. He was a passenger in a purple Mini 1275GT (registration FOX 661L) driven by Gloria Jones as they headed home from Morton's drinking club and restaurant in Berkeley Square. Jones lost control of the car and it struck a sycamore tree after failing to negotiate a small humpback bridge near Gipsy Lane on Queens Ride, Barnes, southwest London. Bolan died instantly, while Gloria Jones suffered a broken arm and jaw.

BLODWYN PIG

Towards the end of my time as CEO at College Ents, I received a phone call from the Blodwyn Pig management. That call gave me a big hint that it was time to get out of the agency business.

The Blodwyn Pig office requested that my agency supplies a photo of a topless prepubliscent girl that they planned to feature on their next LP cover.

I thought, 'What the fuck I am doing in a business that wants me to supply a picture of a young nude girl that will be paedophile in content.'

Blodwyn Pig were a British blues–rock group founded by guitarist–vocalist–songwriter Mick Abrahams, after he left Jethro Tull in 1968 due to a falling-out with Tull leader Ian Anderson.

Abrahams wishing to stay close to Jethro Tull's blues and jazz roots, Anderson wishing to develop less overt blues and jazz material. He left Jethro Tull after their debut album, *This Was*, was released, and formed Blodwyn Pig with Jack Lancaster (saxophone), Andy Pyle (bass guitar), and Ron Berg (drums); future Yes and Flash guitarist Peter Banks became one of several guitarists to succeed Abrahams after he left to form his own band for a time.

With Abrahams and Lancaster in the lead, Blodwyn Pig recorded two albums, *Ahead Rings Out* in 1969 and *Getting To This* in 1970. Both reached the Top Ten of the UK

Albums Chart and charted in the United States; *Ahead Rings Out* displayed a jazzier turn on the heavy blues–rock that formed the band's core rooted in the British 1960s rhythm and blues scene from which sprang groups like The Yardbirds, Free and eventually Led Zeppelin.

Saxophonist–singer Lancaster as prominent in the mix as Abrahams; some critics thought this contrast bumped the band toward a freer, more experimental sound on the second album.

The group became something of a favourite on the underground concert circuit.
I told them that I had no intention of supplying a photo print of a topless prepubliscent girl, planned for their next LP cover.

LONG JOHN BALDRY

I was a rock music agent during all of John Baldry's musical incarnations. I booked the Alexis Korner's Blues Incorporated when he was lead singer. And then again with Cyril Davies R&B All Stars which led to the fabulous Long John Baldry and his Hoochie Coochie Men.

And as the leader of The Steampacket he, unknowingly, saved my bacon. Remember, they filled the void at the R C A when the Pink Floyd were unavailable for that Royal Music Extravaganza.

John William "Long John" Baldry, 12 January 1941 – 21 July 2005, was an English and Canadian blues singer and a voice actor. He sang with many British musicians, with Rod Stewart and Elton John appearing in bands led by Baldry in the 1960s.

He enjoyed pop success in the UK where *Let the Heartaches Begin* reached No. 1 in 1967. Baldry lived in Canada from the late 1970s until his death. There he continued to make records and do voiceover work. He was the voice of Dr. Robotnik in *Adventures of Sonic the Hedgehog*.

Born John William Baldry in England, he grew to 6ft 7in (2.01m) that resulted in the nickname "Long John".

He was one of the first British vocalists to sing blues in clubs. John appeared quite regularly in the early '60s in the Gyre and Gymble coffee lounge, around the corner from Charing Cross railway station. He sometimes appeared at Eel Pie Island, on the Thames at Twickenham and at the Station Hotel in Richmond, one of the Rolling Stones' earliest gigs.

Baldry was openly gay during the early 1960s when homosexuality was still criminalised. Baldry supported Elton John in coming to terms with his own sexuality.

In 1978 his then-upcoming album *Baldry's Out* announced his formal coming out, and he addressed sexuality issues with a cover of Canadian songwriter Bill Amesbury's "A Thrill's a Thril".

GRAHAM BOND ORGANISATION

Graham John Clifton Bond, 28 October 1937 – 8 May 1974, was an English musician, considered a founding father of the English rhythm and blues boom of the 1960s. Graham worked for me throughout the 1960's culminating in that Royal Performance at the RCA in 1967.

Bond was an innovator, described as "an important, under-appreciated figure of early British R&B" along with Cyril Davies and Alexis Korner. Jack Bruce, John McLaughlin and Ginger Baker first achieved prominence in his group, the Graham Bond Organisation. Bond was voted Britain's New Jazz Star in 1961. His albums included "The Sound of '65" and "There's A Bond Between Us". As such he was a major influence upon later rock keyboardists: Deep Purple's Jon

Lord said "*He taught me, hands on, most of what I know about the Hammond organ*".

Adopted from a Dr. Barnardo's home, Bond was educated at the Royal Liberty School in Gidea Park, East London, where he learned music.
He first gained attention as a jazz saxophonist as a member of the Don Rendell Quintet, then briefly joined Alexis Korner's Blues Incorporated before forming the Graham Bond Quartet with musicians he met in the Korner group, Ginger Baker on drums and Jack Bruce on double bass, together with John McLaughlin on guitar. He became the Graham Bond Organization.

Lack of commercial success, plus internal struggles, brought an end to the group in 1967 as Bond's mental and physical health deteriorated.

Jack Bruce and Ginger Baker had already left, to form Cream with Eric Clapton. Baker's replacement, Jon Hiseman, and Dick Heckstall-Smith went on to form Colosseum

On May 8 1974, Bond died under the wheels of a train at Finsbury Park station, London at the age of 36. Most sources list the death as a suicide. Friends agree that he was off drugs, although becoming increasingly obsessed with the occult.

DAVID BOWIE - LEGEND

David agreed to compere our "Search" rock music event at the Lyceum in the Strand. He helped organize the event in the afternoon and then brilliantly compered it in the evening.
We had floated the idea of the competition initially to both the Melody Maker and N M E. The Melody Maker immediately ran with it. They agreed to give 'Search' a big launch.
 We arranged for the heats to be judged by local student union officials throughout England.

Bowie had worked hard, and spent a period of time knocking on various recording company doors. At one time, he changed managers more often than his socks. He was determined to get the best people around him. David's recording of Space Oddity, is on my best ever list. It was first released in 1969 and went to No 5 here in the UK. However, the record eventually made it to No 1 in 1975. It had taken 6 years and 63 days to reach the peak. The slowest record to top the charts of all time.

David undertook a period of experimentation. He re-emerged during the glam rock era as the flamboyant,

androgynous alter ego Ziggy Stardust. He released "Starman" and the album "The Rise and Fall of Ziggy Stardust", "Spiders from Mars". Biographer David Buckley commented, "(Bowie) challenged the core belief of the rock music of its day" and "created the biggest cult…" The Ziggy persona was one facet of a career marked by continual reinvention.
Also musical innovation and striking visual presentation. Several years before David had added a vital skill to his act by joining Lindsay Kemp's mime company. That unique experience helped him towards presenting various musical incarnations.

Only a genius like Bowie could transform himself into a musical chameleon. David adapted his career to the whims and changes of a fickle, yet appreciative, audience. Who could transcend the musical divide between the comic Laughing Gnome and the iconic Ziggy Stardust?

Who would have the vigor and courage to recite 'The Lord's Prayer' to a hedonistic rock festival audience? Only David Bowie.

CHICKEN SHACK

I liked this group very much. I went to their performances on many occasions. They were all at gigs that I had booked. They played my kind of music.

Chicken Shack are a British blues band, founded in the mid-1960s by Stan Webb (guitar and vocals), Andy Silvester (bass guitar), and Alan Morley (drums), who were later joined by Christine Perfect (vocals and keyboards) in 1968.

Stan Webb and Andy Sylvester formed Sounds of Blue in 1964 as a Stourbridge-based r'n'b band.

The band also included Christine Perfect and Chris Wood (later to join Traffic) amongst others in their line up. With a change of line-up in 1965 they changed their name to Chicken Shack, naming themselves after Jimmy Smith's *Back at the Chicken Shack* album.

'Chicken shacks' (chicken restaurants) had also by then frequently been mentioned in blues and rhythm and blues songs, as in Amos Milburn's hit, "Chicken Shack Boogie". They made their first U.K appearance at the 1967 National Jazz and Blues Festival, Windsor and released "Forty Blue Fingers, Freshly Packed and Ready to Serve" in early 1968.

Chicken Shack only enjoyed modest commercial success, although they had two minor hits with "I'd Rather Go Blind" and

"Tears In The Wind", after which Perfect left the band in 1969 when she married John McVie of Fleetwood Mac.
Webb reformed the band as a trio with John Glascock on bass and Paul Hancox on drums, and they recorded *Imagination Lady.*

The line-up didn't last; Glascock left to join Jethro Tull, while Webb was recruited for Savoy Brown in 1974 and recorded the album *Boogie Brothers* with them.
From 1977 until the present Webb has revived the Chicken Shack name on a number of occasions, with a rotating membership over a 30 year period of British blues musicians including, at various times, Paul Butler, Keef Hartley, ex-Ten Years After drummer Ric Lee and Miller Anderson. The band has remained popular as a live attraction in Europe

CHERRY PICKERS STEEL BAND

The leader of this steel band was a good friend of mine. Max Cherrie was a great musician and a super guy. I arranged for the production of their album at EMI records. They recorded at the famous Abbey Road studios. I also named and published some of the tracks from that album. These included 'Early Morning', 'Meridian' and 'Afternoon Tea'.
I have an added affection for the band

because of a dreadful fatal van smash on a motorway, returning from a gig. As a tribute to Max I list below some questions and answers with regard to forming a steel band.

What instruments would a music teacher need to make a small steel band?

A small steel band would consist of :- 1 ENGINE ROOM; 1 SET OF SIX BASSES; 1 SET OF THREE CELLOS; 2 SETS OF TWO SECONDS; 2 SETS OF TWO TENOR PANS.

If this set up is not possible a bass guitar or double bass can be used to fill in the lower section and a keyboard can fill in the harmonies.

How is a drum tuned?

First the drum is emptied, then it is heated and the centre is dropped. Each note is separated using a pummel and map, and the sections are individually tuned with a hammer.

If the section is hit from the underside the note is raised in pitch. If it is hit from above, the note is lowered in pitch.

Does it slip out of pitch regularly?

No, not very often, but when it does slip it needs to go to a tuner.

Don't attempt to tune it yourself.

ERIC CLAPTON

"Would you know my name...?
And I can share your pain...If I saw you in heaven..."

I adore Eric Clapton's fine lyrics. I shared his pain. For me "Tears in Heaven" is the perfect song to help with the grieving process. I have grieved to the point of despair. Eric's song helped me to recover. Eric Patrick Clapton was born in Ripley, Surrey on 30th March 1945.

Eric Clapton grew up with his grandmother, Rose, and her second husband Jack.
After leaving school in 1961, Clapton studied at the Kingston College of Art but was dismissed because his focus remained on music rather than art. He bought his first guitar aged 17 and taught himself. His musical heroes were Big Bill Bronzy, Chuck Berry, and Muddy Waters.
His guitar playing had advanced so far that by the age of 16 people were starting to notice him. Clapton began busking around Kingston, Richmond and the West End of London.

I booked Eric Clapton many times. In the early to mid '60's he was always leaving one group and joining another on a regular basis. We now know that he was searching for the perfect blues sound.

His first band was The Roosters back in 1963. They were around for a short time before he joined Casey Jones and the Engineers. I first booked Eric when he joined The Yardbirds. He replaced Anthony 'Top' Topham. He left the Yardbirds to play blues with John Mayall & the Bluesbreakers. In his one-year stay with Mayall, Clapton gained the nickname "Slowhand" and graffiti in London declared, "Clapton is God." Clapton's output bore the influence of Bob Marley. His version of Marley's "I Shot the Sheriff". Immediately after leaving John Mayall, Clapton formed Cream with drummer Ginger Baker and bassist Bruce. Clapton played sustained blues improvisations and arty, blues-based psychedelic.

He was awarded a CBE for services to music. Eric, a recovering alcoholic and heroin addict, founded the Crossroads Centre on Antigua, a medical facility for recovering substance abusers.

JIMMY CLIFF

I booked Jimmy into colleges via his agent Rik Gunnel. The Gunnel brothers owned the Wardour Street club The Flamingo.

Jimmy performed for Rik in this popular club on a regular basis. Jimmy Cliff is the only currently living musician to hold the Order of Merit, the highest honour that can be granted by the Jamaican government for achievement in the arts and sciences. He is best known among mainstream audiences for songs such as "Sitting in Limbo," "You Can Get It If You Really Want," and "Many Rivers to Cross" from the soundtrack to *The Harder They Come*, which helped popularize reggae across the world;[2] and his covers of Cat Stevens' "Wild World" and Johnny Nash's "I Can See Clearly Now" from the film *Cool Runnings*.

Outside of the reggae world, he is probably best known for his film appearance in *The Harder They Come*. Jimmy Cliff was one of five performers inducted into the Rock and Roll Hall of Fame in 2010.

Cliff was born in Somerton District, St. James, Jamaica. He began writing songs while still at primary school in St. James, listening to a neighbour's sound system. In 1962 his father took him to Kingston to go to Kingston Technical School where he ended up sharing his cousin's one rented room in East Kingston. He sought out many producers while still going to school, trying to get his songs recorded without success.

He also entered talent contests. "One night I was walking past a record store and restaurant as they were closing, pushed myself in and convinced one of them, Leslie Kong, to go into the recording business, starting with me," he writes in his own website biography.

After two singles that failed to make much impression, his career took off when his "Hurricane Hattie" became a hit, while he was aged 14.It was produced by Kong, until his death from a heart attack in 1971. Cliff's later local hit singles included "King of Kings," "Dearest Beverley," "Miss Jamaica," and "Pride and Passion."

COLOSSEUM

The band was formed in September 1968 by drummer Jon Hiseman and tenor sax player Dick Heckstall-Smith. Hiseman and Heckstall-Smith had also previously played in Graham Bond's band. I knew Dick and he was a rare specimen, a brilliant musician and a great bloke.

Bass player Tony Reeves was instrumental in forming *Coliseum*. The musicians had previously worked together in John Mayall's Bluesbreakers on the *Bare Wires* album. Dave Greenslade, on organ, was immediately recruited, and the line-up was completed by Jim Roche on guitar, although Roche only recorded one track before being replaced by James Litherland, (guitar and vocals). The band made their live debut in Newcastle and were promptly recorded by influential BBC Radio 1 DJ John Peel for his *Top Gear* Radio programme. Their first album, *Those Who Are About To Die Salute You*, which opened with the Bond composition "Walkin' in the Park", was released by the Fontana label in 1969, and in March the same year they played at the *Supershow*, a recorded two-day jam session, along with Modern Jazz Quartet, Led Zeppelin, Jack Bruce, Roland Kirk Quartet, Eric Clapton, Steven Stills, and Juicy Lucy. Colosseum's second album, also in 1969, was *Valentyne Suite*, notable as the first release from Vertigo Records. For the third album, *The Grass Is Greener*, released only in the United States in 1970, Dave "Clem" Clempson replaced James Litherland. Louis Cennamo then replaced Tony Reeves on bass, but was replaced by Mark Clarke within a month, and Hiseman recruited vocalist Chris Farlowe to enable Clempson to concentrate on guitar. This lineup had already partly recorded the 1970 album *Daughter of Time*.

In March 1971, the band recorded its concerts at the Big Apple Club in Brighton and at Manchester University. Tracks recorded at Bristol University's Student Union were also used on the live album.

ADGE CUTLER & THE WURZELS

Adge Cutler's band worked for me in several colleges in the mid to late '60's. They were a fun West Country group.
The Wurzels were formed in 1966 as a backing group for, and by, singer/songwriter Adge Cutler.

With a thick Somerset accent, Adge played on his West Country roots, singing many folk songs with local themes such as cider making (and drinking), farming, dung-spreading, local villages and industrial work songs, often with a comic slant.

During the latter half of the 1960s, the band became immensely popular regionally, and the release of the single *Drink Up Thy Zider* in 1966 led to national fame and it reaching number 45 in the UK charts, despite the B-side *Twice Daily* being banned by the BBC for being too raunchy. This was because it told the story of a farm labourer who begins a physical relationship with a female co-worker called 'Lucy Bailey'. The Somerset-based band is best known by many people for their 1976 number one hit "Combine Harvester". "I Am A Cider Drinker", based on the song Una Paloma Blanca, has a history stretching back over 40 years. It is still performed to this day.

The name of the band was dreamed-up by the founder Adge Cutler. It appears to be short for mangelwurzel, a crop grown to feed livestock, and 'wurzel' is also sometimes used in the UK as a synonym for 'yokel'.

The Wurzels' particular "genre" of music was named Scrumpy and Western after the group's first EP of the same name, issued early in 1967. Scrumpy is a name given to traditional Somerset cider. Adge Cutler died after falling asleep at the wheel of his MGB sports car which then overturned on a roundabout approaching the Severn Bridge. He was returning alone from a Wurzels show in Hereford in May 1974. He is buried in Nailsea.

THE SPENCER DAVIS GROUP

The Spencer Davis Group was formed in 1963 in Birmingham when Welsh guitarist Spencer Davis recruited vocalist and organist Steve Winwood and his bass playing brother Muff Winwood. The group was completed with Pete York on drums. Originally called the Rhythm and Blues Quartette, the band performed regularly in the city. In 1964 they signed their first recording contract after Chris Blackwell of Island Records saw them at a local gig.

Blackwell also became their producer. Muff Winwood came up with the band's name, reasoning "Spencer was the only one who enjoyed doing interviews, so I pointed out that if we called it the Spencer Davis Group, the rest of us could stay in bed and let him do them." The group's first professional recording was a cover version of "Dimples", but they came to success at the end of 1965 with "Keep On Running", the group's first number one single. In 1966, they followed this with "Somebody Help Me" and "When I Come Home". They had one single issued in the US on Fontana, as well as "Keep On Running" and "Somebody Help Me" on Atco, but due lack of promotion, none of these 3 singles got airplay or charted.

For the German market the group released "Det war in Schöneberg, im Monat Mai" and "Mädel ruck ruck ruck an meine grüne Seite", Davis having studied in West Berlin in the early 1960s. By the end of 1966 and the beginning of 1967, the group released two more hits, "Gimme Some Lovin'" and "I'm a Man". Both of them sold over one million copies, and were awarded gold record status. These tracks proved to be their two best-known successes, especially in the U.S. In 1966 the group starred in *The Ghost Goes Gear*, a British musical comedy film. It involved the group in a stay at the childhood home of their manager, a haunted manor house in the English countryside.

JULIE DRISCOLL

She and Brian Auger had previously worked in Steampacket, with Long John and Rod Stewart.
Julie really did let it rip that night in 1967 at my gig at the Royal College of Art. She was a star performer in this group. In retrospect The Steampacket have become accepted as the UK's first supergroup.

Julie Tippetts, born Julie Driscoll, 8 June 1947, London, England. She is an English singer and actress, known for her 1960s versions of Bob Dylan's "This Wheel's on Fire", and Donovan's "Season of the Witch", both with Brian Auger & The Trinity.

"This Wheel's on Fire" reached number five in the United Kingdom. With distortion, the imagery of the title and the group's dress and performance, this version came to represent the psychedelic era in British music. Driscoll recorded the song again in the early 90s with Adrian Edmondson as the theme to the BBC comedy series *Absolutely Fabulous*, whose main characters are throwbacks to that era.

Since the 1970s Driscoll has concentrated on experimental vocal music, married jazz musician Keith Tippett and collaborated with him.
Her name is now 'Julie Tippetts', thus using the original spelling of her husband's surname. She participated in Keith Tippett's big band Centipede'

In 1974 she took part in Robert Wyatt's Theatre Royal Drury Lane concert. Julie released a solo album, *Sunset Glow* in 1975. She was lead vocalist on Carla Bley's album *Tropic Appetites* and in John Wolf Brennan's "HeXtet". Later in the 1970s she toured with her own band. She recorded and performed as one of the vocal quartet 'Voice', with Maggie Nichols, Phil Minton and Brian Eley.

DESMOND DEKKER

Whenever I met Desmond at gigs he always gave me a warm Jamaican hug. He was a charming man and a very special artiste. I always loved to watch his performances. There was a rhythmic zing and a certain electric atmosphere whenever he was around.

His recording and publishing directors were at one time members of a group I booked. That group was 'The New Move' and they were led by musicians Bruce White and Tony Cousins, 'The New Move' played for me regularly in Wardour Street, Soho. Bruce and Tony later formed Commercial Entertainments and became very successful. When Bruce White was signing Desmond he confided in me that the situation and negotiations were so tense that he felt like he was ...'sweating blood'. I sold two companies to Bruce. They both made a lot of money. They were Creole Music Ltd and Creole Records Ltd. They published 'Israelites' and made a fortune via PRS.

Desmond Dekker, 16 July 1941 – 25 May 2006, was a Jamaican ska, rocksteady and reggae singer-songwriter and musician. Together with his backing group, The Aces (consisting of Wilson James and Easton Barrington Howard), he had one of the first international Jamaican hits with "Israelites". Other hits include "007 (Shanty Town)" (1967) and "It Miek" (1969). Before the ascent of Bob Marley, Dekker was one of the most popular musicians within Jamaica, and one of its best-known musicians outside it. He took a job as a welder, singing around his workplace while his co-workers encouraged him. In 1961 he auditioned for Coxsone Dodd (Studio One) and Duke Reid (Treasure Isle). Neither was impressed by his talents, and the young man moved on to Leslie Kong's Beverley's record label, where he auditioned before lyrics that resonated with the rude boys starting with one of his best-known songs, "007 (Shanty Town)".

In 1968 Dekker's "Israelites" was released, eventually topping the UK Singles Chart and peaking in the Top Ten of the US Billboard Hot 100. Dekker died of a heart attack at home whilst preparing for a European tour.

EPISODE SIX

Episode Six were much loved by me. They were one of my first group's and played a Soho club residency for my company, Star Attractions, at the St.Moritz club in Wardour Street. They were a real family group. Rehearsing at home, mum giving her views and dad driving them to the gigs.

Episode Six was a British vocal pop-rock group during the mid-1960s. The band was not well known, but foreshadowed the arrival of Deep Purple in the late 1960s.

Episode Six was formed in July 1964 by former members of The Lightnings; Sheila Carter, Graham Carter and Andy Ross, and former members of The Madisons; Roger Glover, Tony Lander and Harvey Shield.

In early 1964 The Lightnings joined my company Star Attractions, and more work came in. They decided to choose a new name and rechristened themselves Episode Six, inspired by a novel called Danish Episode.

The band had already checked out Ian Gillan in a group called Wainwright's Gentlemen and now asked him to join. Prior to this he'd been with The Javelins, a popular local group, from 1961. Ian Gillan's arrival coincided with the band getting a record deal with Pye Records and in July they turned professional, giving up college and jobs. The group split in 1969, the line up then was: John Gustafson, Bass ; Mick Underwood, Drums ; Peter Robinson, Keyboard, Graham Carter, Guitar/ Vocal; Tony Lander, guitar ; Sheila Carter, Organ/ Vocalist.

THE EQUALS

The group were made up of equal white and black musicians. Hence The Equals. I got The Equals a well-paid gig at a college. They had a real good sound and became spectacularly successful. BUT I did not like the attitude of the group's leader Eddy

Grant towards me. I went over to say hello and he gave me the cold shoulder. He looked at me as if I was a white policeman stopping and searching his flashy car. ('Police On My Back'). I resented his attitude. I'd got them a top dollar gig at this college he treated me with contempt.

What a contrast to the love I felt from Desmond Dekker. The Equals were a pop/reggae/rock group that formed in North London, England in 1965. They are mainly remembered for its million-selling chart-topper, "Baby Come Back".

Eddy Grant, then sporting dyed blonde hair, founded the group. Completing the original line-up were John Hall, Pat Lloyd, and twin brothers Derv and Lincoln Gordon. Eddie Grant had health problems and promptly left The Equals to pursue his solo career.

In the late 1970s and early 1980s Grant released several Top 40 singles, including "Living On The Front Line", "Electric Avenue" and "Romancing the Stone". Grant also topped the UK Singles Chart in 1982 with "I Don't Wanna Dance".

Although The Equals never charted again after Grant's departure, they remained a popular live act, performing into the late 1970s and beyond. In 1980, The Clash recorded a cover version of The Equals' song "Police On My Back" (a track from the group's *Baby, Come Back* album).

GEORGIE FAME

Georgie is a fabulously talented musician. I knew him when he started out. I was present when he was band leader for Larry Parnes at a Billy Fury concert at the Trocadero, Elephant & Castle, south London. Georgie Fame, born Clive Powell, 26 June 1943, Leigh, Lancashire, is a British rhythm and blues and jazz singer and keyboard player.
The one-time rock and roll tour musician, who had a string of 1960s hits, is still a popular performer, often working with contemporaries such as Van Morrison and Bill Wyman.

Fame took piano lessons from the age of seven and after leaving Leigh Central County Secondary School at 15, he worked for a brief period in a cotton weaving mill and played piano for a band called The Dominoes in the evenings. He was offered a job by early British rock'n'roll star Rory Blackwell.

At sixteen years of age, Fame went to London and entered into a management agreement with Larry Parnes, who had given new stage names to such artists as Marty Wilde and Billy Fury. Fame later recalled that Parnes had given him an ultimatum over his forced change of name:

" *It was very much against my will but he said,*

'If you don't use my name, I won't use you in the show'. "

Over the following year he toured the UK playing beside Marty Wilde, Joe Brown, Gene Vincent, Eddie Cochran and others. The band was re-billed as "Georgie Fame and the Blue Flames" and went on to enjoy great success. In 1972, Fame married Nicolette (née Harrison), Marchioness of Londonderry, the former wife of the 9th Marquess. Lady Londonderry. Nicolette Powell died in 1993, after jumping off the Clifton Suspension Bridge.

FREE with Paul Kossoff

Paul Francis Kossoff, 14 September 1950 – 19 March 1976, was an English rock guitarist best known as a member of the band Free. He played a gig for me at St.Moritz club in Wardour Street. London. I was the club's *sole agent* for many years.

In April 1968 Kossoff teamed up with Paul

Rodgers (vocals) and Andy Fraser (bass) to form Free. They did the "Transit" circuit for two years and recorded two albums: *Tons of Sobs* (1968) and *Free* (1969). Both albums showcased the band's blues and soul influenced sound. The band played the Isle of Wight festival to both audience and critical acclaim. Sellout tours in the United Kingdom, Europe, and Japan followed, but after the release of the next album, *Highway* (1970), band pressures led to a split. The live album *Free Live*, recorded in 1970, was released in 1971 as a farewell record. While Rodgers and Fraser pursued unsuccessful solo projects, Kossoff and Kirke teamed up with Texan keyboard player John "Rabbit" Bundrick and Japanese bass player Tetsu Yamauchi to release the 1971 album *Kossoff, Kirke, Tetsu and Rabbit*. Free released the album *Free at Last* (1972).

Following its release Fraser decided he had had enough and quit. Kossoff's unhappiness with the end of Free and his drug addictions contributed to a drastic decline in the guitarist's health. On a flight from Los Angeles to New York on 19 March 1976, Kossoff died from drug-related heart problems.

His father, David, was a famous actor. He

was so distraught, at losing his son, that he went on TV and threatened to kill the pusher who supplied the drugs. His grave stone, at Golders Green cemetery, reads: 'All Right Now'.

FAIRPORT CONVENTION

In the late 1960's I came to an agreement with Brunel University. We jointly promoted concerts at the prestigious Lyceum, just off The Strand, London. One of those acts at our concerts was the durable and vastly talented Fairport Convention. They were very popular with lovers of English folk rock music.
The night they played for us, at The Lyceum, it snowed. The audience did not appear because of the cold weather. That is one of the perils of becoming a promoter.

So many things that go wrong can be managed. But the weather is beyond anyone's control. To get the dates at The Lyceum you have to book well in advance. Well ahead of any good or bad weather forecast.

Fairport Convention are an English folk rock and later electric folk band, formed in 1967 who are still touring today. Their original line up was: Simon Nichol, guitar

/ vocals; Richard Thompson guitar/vocals; Ashley Hutchings , bass; Shaun Frater, drums; Judy Dyble, autoharp / vocals.

They are widely regarded as the most important single group in the English folk rock movement.

Their seminal album *Liege and Lief* is generally considered to have launched the electric folk or English folk rock movement, which provided a distinctively English identity to rock music and helped awaken much wider interest in traditional music in general.

The large number of personnel who have been part of the band are among the most highly regarded and influential musicians of their era and have gone on to participate in a large number of significant bands, or enjoyed important solo careers.

CHRIS FARLOWE

Chris Farlowe recorded 'Out of Time' in 1966. It is another one of my favourite tracks. He gigged at several colleges for me. Chris Farlowe, born John Henry Deighton, 13 October 1940, Islington.
He is an English rock, blues and soul singer. He is best known for his hit single

"Out of Time", which rose to #1 in the UK Singles Chart in 1966, and his association with Colosseum and the Thunderbirds. Outside his music career, Farlowe collects war memorabilia.

Inspired by Lonnie Donegan, Farlowe's musical career began with a skiffle group, the John Henry Skiffle Group, in 1957, before he joined the Johnny Burns Rhythm and Blues Quartet, in 1958.
He met guitarist Bob Taylor in 1959 and, through Taylor, joined the Thunderbirds, who went on to record five singles for the Columbia label.

He released a cover version of "Stormy Monday Blues" under the pseudonym of "Little Joe Cook", which perpetuated the myth that he was a black singer. Farlowe moved to Andrew Loog Oldham's Immediate label and recorded eleven singles, five of which were cover versions of Rolling Stones songs including "Paint It, Black", "Think", "Ride On, Baby", "(I Can't Get No) Satisfaction" and "Out of Time".

Farlowe recorded Mike d'Abo's "Handbags and Gladrags". In February 1972 he joined Atomic Rooster, and is featured on the albums Made in England (1972) and Nice 'n' Greasy (1973). He also sang on three tracks from Jimmy Page's Death Wish II soundtrack (1982), as well as the tracks "Hummingbird", "Prison Blues" and "Blues Anthem" on Page's album Outrider (1988). In 2009, Farlowe toured as a featured artist with Maggie Bell and Bobby Tench as part of the Maximum Rhythm and Blues Tour of thirty two UK theatres.

THE FORTUNES

The Fortunes are the good guys.
They honoured their original, low fee, contract with me when they were high in the charts in 1965. The Fortunes are an English harmony beat group. Formed in Birmingham, They first came to prominence and international acclaim in 1965, when "You've Got Your Troubles" broke into the US and UK Top 10s.

Afterwards they had a succession of hits including "Here It Comes Again" and "Here Comes That Rainy Day Feeling Again"; continuing into the 1970s with more globally successful releases such as "Storm in a Teacup" and "Freedom Come, Freedom Go".

Originally formed as a vocal trio backed by an instrumental group known as The Cliftones, the aggregation placed an instrumental track on a compilation album, *Brumbeat*, issued by the local Dial record label. "Cygnet Twitch" (similar to "Saturday Nite at the Duck-Pond" by The Cougars) was a working of Tchaikovsky's "Swan Lake", and they subsequently signed to British Decca in 1963. Their first single, "Summertime, Summertime", was credited to the Fortunes and the Cliftones. However, the vocalists picked up guitars, jettisoned the Cliftones, and added Andy Brown on drums after Mike Redmond — drummer with popular local band the Sunrays — declined their offer, and Dave Carr on keyboards.

The follow-up disc co-written by the singer-songwriter and future Ivy League member Perry Ford, "Caroline", was used as the signature tune for the pirate radio station, Radio Caroline. On 10 January 2008 Rod Allen died after suffering for two months from liver cancer. The remaining members of the band said they would continue touring and recruited The Dakotas lead singer Eddie Mooney.

BILL HAYLEY & THE COMETS

WOW! What an honour. I booked these rock'n'roll icons into the Mistrale Club, Beckenham. I went over to say hello to my hero. My first impression I got was that dumpy Bill Hayley was cross-eyed. The Comets were overweight. However, that did not diminish there rock'n'roll music. They were a real blast from the past. The clubbers loved them. Bill Haley & His Comets were an American rock and roll band that was founded in 1952 and continued until Haley's death in 1981.

The band, also known by the names Bill Haley and The Comets and Bill Haley's Comets was the earliest group of white musicians to bring rock and roll to the attention of white America and the rest of the world. Bandleader Bill Haley had previously been a country music performer; after recording a country and western-styled version of "Rocket 88", a rhythm and blues song, he changed musical direction to a new sound which came to be called rock and roll.

With his spit curl and the band's matching plaid dinner jackets and energetic stage behaviour, many fans consider them to be as revolutionary in their time as The Beatles or the Rolling Stones were a decade or two later. In 1953 Haley scored his first national success with an original song called "Crazy Man, Crazy", a phrase Haley said he heard from his teenage audience.

Haley later claimed the recording sold a million copies. "Crazy Man, Crazy" was the first rock and roll song to be televised nationally when it was used on the soundtrack for a 1953 television play starring James Dean. Haley and His Comets then recorded *"Rock Around the Clock",* Haley's biggest hit, and one of the most important records in rock and roll history. Sales of *"Rock Around the Clock"* started slow but eventually sold an estimated 25 million copies.

LED ZEPPELIN

THEIR DEBUT GIG WAS FOR ME…
IT CAN'T GET MUCH BETTER THAN THAT.

Luckily Peter Grant gave me the opportunity to be the first rock music agent to book Led Zeppelin.

It was an amazing set of circumstances, some would say pure synchronicity. This is how I came to book Led Zep on the very first gig.

What an honour.

"Hi! Is that Peter?"

"Yeah! Who's that?" I did not immediately recognise the voice on the phone.

"Peter Grant. Look I've got something special for you. You were one of my best agents for The Yardbirds. They've just completed some European dates as The New Yardbirds, some dates they were contracted to complete. They have now become Led Zeppelin and I'm giving you the chance to be the first agent to book them."

Peter explained about the demise of The Yardbirds...told me about the change of name and new line up. He explained he needed a few dates to launch the band on the UK

"Thanks Peter", I said "I will do my best. I'll call you back if I get anything."

Within a couple of hours, I received a call from the social secretary at Surrey University.

I casually mentioned Led Zeppelin and I could feel the gasp of excitement at the end of the phone.

"But they are going to be massive. How much do you want?"
I quoted the fee and he gave me a series of dates for Peter to choose from. I got back to Peter Grant and Led Zeppelin's

first ever gig was contracted. They went down a storm. I could not make it that night as I was already booked to attend another gig. Much less important but I had given my word.

LED ZEPPELIN DEBUT

LED ZEPPELIN, the group formed by Jimmy Page after the disbandment of the Yardbirds, make their debut at Surrey University tomorrow (Friday).

Their manager, Peter Grant, is currently finalising a six-week American tour for the group, starting around November 16.

They have started work on their first LP which will be released early in the New Year.

LEDZEPPELIN.COM

Yardbirds Goodbye

The Yardbirds make their farewell London appearance at the Marquee Club tonight (Friday) and their final performance is set for Liverpool University tomorrow (Saturday) — after which the group disbands. Leader Jimmy Page has now decided to name his new group Led Zeppelin, and this will make its stage debut in late October.

The new group has already cut a single and LP for early December release, and it was announced this week that Led Zeppelin has been signed by Harold Davison.

LEDZEPPELIN.COM

There is a 'recollection' by a former student that the gig was in Battersea. Much of the Guildford site was still a building site.

This person signs as anonymous.

Here is that letter:

"Re Surrey University

The concert WAS in Battersea, I was there!
Battersea College of Advanced Technology received its charter to become the University of Surrey in 1966.

The new campus was being built in Guildford and in 1968 the University became a 'split personality' when half of the departments moved to Guildford for the start of that academic year!

This was the first big concert of the Autumn Term and a lot of people came up from Guildford for it so it was quite a reunion. I didn't realise the momentousness of the occasion at the time…"

PINK FLOYD

Syd Barrett left the group soon after the residency gig they did for me at The Royal College of Art, Kensington in 1967…

Pink Floyd was the most successful group to emerge from the underground scene. They had hitherto played gigs at the Marquee and the Roundhouse.

They also performed regularly at the UFO club, the club that promoted the flourishing hippy theme. Pink Floyd also appeared regularly at Middle Earth.
After signing to new management, Peter Jenner & Andrew King, the group secured a contract with EMI. The first single was Syd Barrett's 'Arnold Layne'. A transvestite who steals underwear. This track reached number 20 in the UK charts.

The follow up single 'See Emily Play' reached number 6. Their first Album was entitled 'The Piper at The Gates of Dawn'. Many tracks on the L P featured compositions by Syd Barrett. His authority in Pink Floyd waned after he fell under the heavy influence of hallucinogens. David Gilmour replaced Barrett in 1968

THE SHIRALEE

I loved this fabulous '60's band. So together, so reliable and such fun. The Shiralee were a West London based band formed in February 1965 originally named

"The Albert Square". The line-up was Ken Golding (singer), Case Cummings (rhythm guitar), Bernie Clark (bass guitar) Graham Barnes (lead guitar) and Mick Nolan (drums).

The band learnt their trade by regularly playing five nights a week, including long performances at American Air Force Bases across South East England.

In 1967 they changed their name to "The Shiralee" and released their single "I Will Stay By Your Side" on the Fontana label. The B-side "Penny Wren" was written by Bernie Clark about a girl he had met at one of their gigs at the London Naval Base "HMS President". "Penny Wren" was played on popular BBC radio programme "Two Way Family Favourites". Both tracks proudly produced by me.

To promote the record the band appeared live on BBC radio with DJ Johnny Cash and Paul Jones from Manfred Mann. It was reviewed by Brian Matthew on his Friday night radio show and frequently played as a 'climber' on pirate Radio London as well as achieving some chart success in Sweden.

Soon after the record's release Bernie

Clark and Mick Nolan both left the band and Pete Reichardt joined as the new drummer, with Case Cummings switching from rhythm guitar to take over the role of bass player. To complete the new line-up Tim Wallace was brought in as keyboard player. The band built up quite a following playing at clubs, colleges and corporate events.

They supported chart acts including 'Lulu', 'Jimmy Cliff', 'Cliff Bennett', 'Gino Washington', 'The Swinging Blue Jeans", 'The Nashville Teens', 'The Easybeats' etc. After five hectic but enjoyable years on the road The Shiralee disbanded in December 1969. Gone but never ever forgotten.

ROGER SPEAR'S GIANT KINETIC WARDROBE.

Roger was featured with The Bonzo Dog Doo Dah Band in the ITV show 'Do Not Adjust Your Set'.
Roger toured extensively (and tirelessly) with his solo show Roger Ruskin Spear and his Giant Kinetic Wardrobe (aka Giant Orchestral Wardrobe).

A feature of this was a female tailor's dummy fitted with proximity switches, which produced increasingly high-pitched screams when a hand neared her chest. Roger formed Tatty Ollity with Dave Glasson, former Member of Bob Kerr's Whoopee Band, Sam Spoons and Dave Knight (now deceased).

They released a single, 'Punktuation' on the Rough Trade label. In 1982 (from November 3), Roger took part in the new Channel 4's 'Cut Price Comedy Show', a weekly confection of corny sketches and ironic, end-of-the-pier fun. As a critic puts it: 'the Cut Price Comedy Show was an (intentionally) corny sketch series with a heavy dependence on the kind of 'jokes' you'd find on an ice cream stick and a budget that seemed to have been scraped together from copper coins found in the gutter outside the studio.

But that was the point - the title made it clear that it was going to be penny-pinching, barrel-scraping stuff, right? Trouble is it didn't make it as critic-proof as you might think, and the tabloid scribes fell over themselves to scold the then new channel for squandering airtime on something so bereft of invention.
Some people just don't get irony.

ROD STEWART

Rod is a marvel. What a fantastic voice.

What a performer. He is the DADDY of them all. (No pun Rod. Honest!)

But for years he was a singing apprentice learning his trade.

He was playing with a small rock'n'blues combo who played many of the London beat clubs around at that time.

Rod was working for me on a regular Tuesday night gig in Wardour Street at La Discothèque.

I had already booked Rod on a number of previous occasions. He had worked for me when he was featured with Jimmy Powell and the Dimensions.

Rod started recording for Decca records in the early 60's. He released "Good Morning Little Schoolgirl" on the Decca label in 1964.

Rod was also second vocalist in John Baldry's 'Hoochie Coochie Men' who played for me at many college gigs. Rod went on to become one of the most loved singers of several generations. It was Rod who fronted The Steampacket with Long John Baldry on that famous night in 1967. The night he saved my rock music business.

The night when Rod, Long John, Julie, Elton and Brian et al saved my ass by playing this royal gig for H.M. The Queen at The Royal College of Art.

Everyone originally wanted Pink Floyd but really enjoyed the blasting rasping music of Steam packet even more. Rod and his musical mates made it one hell of a night to remember…forever.
Thanks.

THE YARDBIRDS

One of the last gigs The Yardbirds played for me was, ironically, at the Last Chance Saloon in Oxford Street. The 'Last Chance' had ornate mirrors along the walls and a whiff of eastern incense permeated throughout the club. It felt like being in an extravagant Turkish brothel.

The Yardbirds had previously had a residency at the Crawdaddy Club in Richmond. The Last Chance Saloon did not provide a cult following. The members there were the sort that every generation throws up. The Nouvous riche, show offs, high society dropouts and their common girlfriends. They were there to preen and be seen. Not the type who would appreciate that the Yardbirds were to have an immense influence on the future of the British music scene. The Yardbirds are now thought of as one the legends of British rock. I had booked The Yardbirds many times since they were formed in 1963. That original line up was Keith Relf, vocals, harmonica; Anthony 'Top' Topham, guitar; Chris Dreja, guitar; Paul Samuel – Smith, bass; Jim McCarty, drums.

Peter Grant, their road manager at the time, was big hulk of a man with shrewd eyes. Always check the eyes, the mirror of any soul. I remember him puffing and panting as he heaved the heavy equipment down to the semi basement club. I walked passed Peter on my way to say hello to the club owner. For some reason Peter just glared at me. I still don't know why. Perhaps he thought I should help him lug the equipment.

When he became their manager he pursued an innovative approach. "When I started managing The Yardbirds, they weren't getting the hit singles, but were on the college circuit and underground scene in America. Instead of trying to get played on Top 40 radio, I realised that there was another market. We were the first UK act to get booked at places like The Fillmore. The scene was changing."

As mentioned he started as a doorman at the famous 2i's coffee bar in Old Compton street. Peter "G" Grant later managed several well-known groups. He has been described as "one of the shrewdest and most ruthless managers in rock history". He later managed several well-known groups, many of whom I regularly booked. These included Jeff Beck, The New Vaudeville Band, Bad Company, Maggie Bell and The Nashville Teens. Peter later became a record executive for Swan Song Records.

THE WHO
They came into my life as The High Numbers a couple of years after I had opened my first rock agency, Star Attractions. I was holding auditions for a group to take up a residency when these four mods whooshed in. They very quickly did their audition set and then whooshed out again. All so fast. No fuckin' messing about for these ambitious lads. I did not book them on this occasion.

The Who started life as the Detours. Pete Townshend and John Entwistle were still at Acton County Grammar School when they joined Daltrey's band. After a few musical membership shakeups, the group line up was Pete Townshend, guitar, keyboards, vocals. Roger Daltrey, vocals. John Entwistle, bass, horns and vocals. Keith Moon, drums.

After a mix of managers, they eventually signed to Kit Lambert and Terence Stamp. It was then that things began to happen. Kit had seen the group, under the name High

Numbers, at the Railway Hotel in Harrow.

Kit and Terence persuaded the group to change their name to The Who again. Pete Townhend smashed his first guitar at The Railway. Smash them! Destroy them! We are the new generation, so take notice!

I thought it economically unviable when I witnessed the smashing of genuine instruments in their final set at my gig at The London College of Printing. Their managers, Kit Lambert and Chris Stamp, had cleverly crafted this as part of a publicity campaign. It certainly worked.

I went to the college and watched in awe, with all the students, at the smashing of instruments in their final set. Teenagers could identify with the outrage of the established order of things. Smash and Destroy. We are the new generation, so take notice! I thought it economically unviable when I witnessed the smashing of genuine instruments in their final set. Their managers, Kit Lambert and Chris Stamp, had cleverly crafted this as part of a publicity campaign. The publicity worked.

It was successful because their fans could identify with the angst perpetuated by their own anger and outrage. Smash and destroy was the way to spread the word to the record buying teenagers. It became a trademark finale to their performances.

This fitted neatly into one of Kit's philosophies of life, *'Just to succeed in life is banal to the point of failure. The purpose of success is to have something substantial to wreck. And the ultimate triumph is to create a magnificent disaster.'*

Kit described their first meeting, *"I shall always remember that night we first saw them together. I had never seen anything like it. The Who have a hypnotic effect on an audience. I realized that the first time I saw them. It was like a black mass. Even then, Pete Townshend was doing all that electronic feedback stuff. Keith Moon was going wild on the drums. The effect on the audience was tremendous. It was as if they were in a trance. They just sat there watching or shuffled around the dance floor, awestruck."*

A couple of years after they signed with Kit I received an enquiry from a south London college.
So I phoned Kit at his office about this possible booking. He was in fine acerbic form.

"Kit Lambert. What can I do for you?"

"Hello, it's Peter at Star Attractions. I've got a booking for The Who at The London College of Printing. I want to check some dates."

"Star what?"

"Star Attractions!"

Kit then loudly announced to his management company colleagues, "Hey, this lot are called Star Attractions. Ha ha ha Star Attractions…What do you want?"

I then proceeded to agree a fee and arrange the booking. The instrument smashing initially bemused the students at the London College of Printing in Elephant and Castle. As mentioned, I thought it was economic madness. How wrong could I be? Teenagers could identify with the outrage and non-acceptance of the established order of things. Smash them! Destroy them! We are the new generation, so take notice!

Kit Lambert and Chris Stamp had cleverly crafted the instrument smashing as part of a publicity campaign. The publicity worked. But at what financial cost? Those instruments were genuine and pricey.

Teenagers of every ilk could identify with the angst perpetuated by the outrage. Anger carried by every new generation against parents, elders and the fuckin' established order of things. Smash them! Destroy them! We have arrived and to prove it we're The Who!

The group start a residency at London's Marquee Club in 1964. The shows soon become sell-outs, but the equipment smashing was taking a toll on the group's finances. There was no cheating on the backs of cheap fake instruments.

In the late 1960's I teamed up with Essex businessman Anton. He and I started together promoting a few bands at the now famous Circus Tavern. Anton also introduced me to freemasonry, which at the time enthralled me. Many years later, I told my children that I if I told any Mason secrets then my tongue would be cut out and my throat slit. The thought of that fascinated them for years.

I ceased being a Freemason when I became a Catholic. This was to enable me to marry the love of my life, Mary, in a Catholic church. In those days Freemasons did not welcome Catholics. However, they are welcome now. I was asked to rejoin the St James' Lodge, next door to Rupert Murdoch's London home. I declined their kind invitation.

We planned a Rock Music Festival in

Anton's manor. His family were well known, they ran a successful local business. My job was to arrange, book the groups and produce. Anton would finance, organise and get the field from the farmer. So I checked out all available rock acts to head the festival. Amen Corner and The Who were both available. HOWEVER, they both wanted top billing. What a headache!

Amen Corner had recently been top of the charts with 'Half as Nice', featuring Andy Fairweather-Low. They were current big timers. The Who would eventually become a legend in their own lifetimes but were not flavour of the month at this time. But they refused to be second on the bill to Amen Corner.

I could not get any other rock attraction that would sell tickets in quantity. I was tortured in my negotiations for the two to appear together without solving the billing problem on the posters. After three days and nights of torment I eventually received a call from a colleague who had the solution. It was simple.

In a square box on the poster you drew a line from the top left hand corner to the bottom right hand corner. This gave you two rectangles each side. The left hand side was first but the right hand side was top. It was perfect. Both groups agreed to this billing solution. The show could go ahead.

If you ever get involved with promoting a music festival then get the experts with proven track records. Anton was busy with his other business interests. I was flat out running a busy rock music agency that took all my time and more.

We let others get on with the set up. A big mistake.
The lighting guy found it difficult to cope. We nearly did not have a festival. Other problems were mounting but the main one was down to us. We picked the farmer's field too far from public transport drop offs.

Hundreds of people were searching for our festival on the day. Eventually most found us. Location, location, location sums up festival positioning as well as property buying.
And then we had a devastating problem on the night of the festival. One of The Who broke his arm and could not perform. We did not have a riot because The Who appeared at the festival and explained to the crowd exactly what had befallen their injured member. Amen Corner went down well and saved the day as did all support groups. I will always be grateful to The Who, they cared enough to appear and tell the

audience exactly why they could not perform. They were, and always will be, a great rock band.

Because of the Who's nonperformance we broke even. If the Who had played we would have lost a fortune, even in those dim and distant days the Who were not cheap to book. On this occasion they appeared free of charge to tell the audience personally of their misfortune and save a riot.

Hours earlier, just about mid-morning, when we were arranging the first set ups for the support bands I spotted this gorgeous roadie. She was truly beautiful. We were chatting and I discovered she was on the bounce. She'd had a major bust up with her muso boyfriend and they split. Permanently. She wanted me to give her a hug...and more. In spite of my overwhelming desires, I did nothing about it. I was married with a beautiful daughter aged two. I stayed faithful.

After Anton and I had paid Amen Corner and all the ancillary services, including the lighting clown, we ended up breaking even. Just. Ironically, because the Who could not play, we did not lose too much money. They did not even charge us for travelling expenses. If they had played we would have lost a small fortune.

Fate.

Support groups

All the big name rock artistes enjoyed our bookings at colleges throughout the UK. Rod said recently that he loved touring the college circuit. It was rewarding both artistically and financially. The gig supplied an intelligent, appreciative, and captive audience, who buy the records. And probably become life long fans. And the fees I negotiated were the best.

Colleges always paid top dollar and got the stars they wanted. They put on a headliner with a support group. I usually supplied both. The top biller costing lots, and the support? Fifteen to twenty five pounds.

I once received a call from an executive at N E M S enterprises. This was Brian Epstein's London 'Beatles Company'. Brian's link with NEMS Enterprises (North End Music Stores) started when Brian's father, Harry, started to employ Brian in the record department of his store. It was the newly-opened NEMS music department on Great Charlotte Street, Liverpool. Epstein worked "day and night" at the store to make it a success, and it became one of the biggest musical retail outlets in the North of England. The

Epsteins opened a second store at 12–14 Whitechapel, and Brian Epstein was put in charge of the entire operation. On 3 August 1961, Epstein started a regular music column in the *Mersey Beat* magazine, called 'Record Releases by Brian Epstein of NEMS'. After discovering The Beatles and other Merseyside acts he moved to prestigious offices in central London.

The **NEMS** (Beatles) executive offered £25.00 per support group for a series of Sunday concerts at The Prince of Wales Theatre, Piccadilly. Supports did not do the gigs for the money. They did them for the valuable exposure and publicity. Worth its weight in gold for possible future fame and fortune.

DAVID BOWIE – ROCK ICON

#TRACK 4
- Search –
With David Bowie

What a fantastic performer.
What an icon.
David is also a superb songwriter.
David has that double X factor and
David hosted my presentation of the competition "Search".

It was held at The Lyceum and Melody Maker sponsored it.

< " SEARCH FOR THE GHOST OF THE SOUL OF ROCK MUSIC "

In the late 1960's College Ents entered into an agreement with that popular and renowned music paper. It was to organize a talent competition for up and coming rock groups on the college circuit. We arranged for groups to audition in colleges the length and breadth of the UK circuit. David transferred his performance skills to this project and changed it from a potential failure to a fantastic success.

Back in the sixties everything was cool and new! Our parents had lived through, and we had grown up in, the apprehensive forties and boring fifties. The only good thing about the fifties was the coming of the Lord. The king of Rock'n'Roll: Elvis 'Before Elvis there was nothing.' (John Lennon and me)

In the sixties everybody was on the musical bandwagon. Newspaper publishers were making a mint with their music papers: Merseybeat, Disc, New Record Mirror, Melody Maker and New Musical Express. The Melody Maker was a little grander than the others. It was the weekly for the Jazz and 'serious' rock fraternity. It came in at the quality end of the market.

Writing about jazz musicians, big bands and rock groups rather than 'popcorn' groups. Their readers was purchased erudite well produced L P records. They thought of themselves as true music fans. The pop fraternity were the plebs.

I had a guy working for me at College Ents called John. He was tall, good looking with long 60's style hair (blowin' in the wind). His mother was Irish and either she or he had kissed the Blarney stone. Anyway John had some good ideas and the gift of the gab.

The ideas came to him while he was sitting on the toilet which was situated at the back of my office. He sat on that toilet for what seemed like ages.

I excused myself from my office when I had an important meeting. Listening to farting and other toilet noises was not conducive to talking business with the managers of The Hollies or The Yardbirds.

I know you are expecting me to say that his ideas dreamt up in that Archer Street toilet were crap. But I won't because they were not all crap. Only most of them.

Anyway he rushed out of the loo one mid-morning, he always got up late and therefore did not have time to go to the bathroom at home. He started shouting eureka or some such thing. He had come up with the idea for unknown groups, who played the college circuit, to take part in a competition. The winner would get a recording contract and a large spread in a music paper. The plan was great and the publicity generated for College Ents would be even better. I will always be grateful to him for that fabulous idea. The winner would get a recording contract, continuous publicity and a management / agency contract with us.

We floated the idea to both the Melody Maker and NME. The Melody Maker loved the idea.
After several meetings with young music journos in smoke filled cafes, over fried egg and chips, in and around Fleet Street the plan was formulated.

Melody Maker eventually designated a senior reporter, Chris Welch, to put the story and event together with us. We all met him in a 'greasy spoon' café in Fleet Street. All the cafes and milk bars were busy in Fleet Street in those days.

The majority of newspapers and news agencies operated from that famous street at that time. The Fleet Street pubs were friendly, smokey and much frequented by boozy male journalists' morning, noon and night.

Journos always enjoyed a drink or three. In those days their favourite pub was an extension to their office. A lot of the news stories were written up in the cozy, familiar and noisy saloon bars full of cigar and cigarette smoke and bawdy chatter.

Because I didn't want alcohol getting in the way of our negotiations I insisted we met in a Fleet Street café. The meeting was affable to begin with. But during negotiations I asked for a guarantee of maximum exposure. I proposed that 'Search' should get prominent coverage on the front and right hand pages.

I was warned not to press our claims too aggressively. If I was too demanding then the MM editor had the power to cancel the project. I was reminded that 'Search' would only succeed on a national basis if Melody Maker was involved. And we had to accept that the editor was God and we had to obey and respect his every whim. In the circumstances I decided to keep stum and we made the best deal we could get. We eventually came up with a contract and a demarcation of responsibilities.

We celebrated by enjoying a greasy all day breakfast, including mushrooms, fatty bacon and fried bread. No black pudding thank you.

We washed this down with coffee made with a spoonful of Nescafe, hot water and milk. None of your fancy coffees in those days. It was the era of the chipped mug.

We negotiated a deal which we at College Ents were very happy with. My assistant and I went on to organize regional rounds for the competition.
The Melody Maker faithfully covered all events in a prominent part of the paper. All the regional winners went to the final held in London.

'Search' would be announced in the Melody Maker and we would spread the word around the colleges to encourage unknown rock bands to take part. The response was good and area heats were arranged. Local Student Union officials voted for their favourites. The Final was to be in London at that very fine venue where the Strand meets Aldwych. It was The Lyceum and that is where David comes in. I had to find a 'rock name' that would add gravitas to the proceedings.

David Bowie was making a famous name for himself. I convinced my team and Melody Maker that David was our stand out star host for the 'Search' final. David and his manager agreed. Not least because it would help cement and promote his image with the influential student market. David had worked hard to achieve fame. He'd spent a period of time knocking on various recording company doors. At one time, he changed managers frequently. He was determined to get the best people around him to further his career. David's recording of Space Oddity, is on my best ever list. It was first released in 1969 and went to No 5 here in the UK. However, the record eventually made it to No 1 in 1975. It had taken 6 years and 63 days to reach the peak. The slowest record to top the charts of all time.

After the 1969 release of "Space Oddity" David undertook a period of experimentation. He re-emerged during the glam rock era as the flamboyant, androgynous alter ego Ziggy Stardust.
He released "Starman" and the album The Rise and Fall of Ziggy Stardust and the Spiders from Mars. Biographer David Buckley commented, "(Bowie) challenged the core belief of the rock music of its day" and "created perhaps the biggest cult…" The Ziggy persona was one facet of a career marked by continual reinvention, musical innovation and striking visual presentation.

Several years before David had added a

vital skill to his act by joining Lindsay Kemp's mime company. That unique experience helped him to present various musical incarnations.

Only a genius like Bowie could transform himself into a musical chameleon. David adapted his career to the whims and changes of a fickle, yet appreciative, audience. Who could transcend the musical divide between the comic Laughing Gnome and the iconic Ziggy Stardust? Who would have the vigor and courage to recite 'The Lord's Prayer' to a hedonistic rock festival audience? Only David Bowie.

I originally found the Lyceum theatre cavernous, uninspiring and lacking in any atmosphere. The place reminded me of a huge barn. That was back in the sixties. Today the venue is bright and successful. Walt Disney's 'The Lion King' has transformed it far beyond my dreary recollections.

At the start of proceedings I was in a bad mood, my team had let me down. This mood was exacerbated because our strategic rehearsal plans was badly constructed. And the 'Search' competition could crash on the night unless we restructured immediately.

The team had drawn up a technical rehearsal schedule that was badly prepared. I had relied on my usually reliable team to complete a professional schedule. I do however take some responsibility; I had focused too much on the marketing, publicity and promotional side of the event. The big worry was that my Melody Maker partners would discover the weak link. If they got wind of the bad planning there would be hell to pay. I would be held responsible and embarrassed by the episode.

The Lyceum has a capacity to hold an audience of 2000 patrons. The perfect number to create that perfect warm theatre atmosphere. The Old Lyceum Theatre was first built in 1765. In the late 18th century Charles Dibdin supplied musical entertainment. Back then it was music of a different kind, rock'n'roll made its entrance some 200 years later.

In the past, the theatre had featured a circus. I certainly didn't want the rehearsals turning into a circus with me and the staff being the clowns. But with so many groups, and their equipment, getting in each other's way, I wouldn't bet against it. The requirement had been to plan a logistics model that would create a dream rehearsal. A prearranged set up schedule should have been communicated to all finalists prior to them arriving at the Lyceum. It wasn't and I blamed myself.

Happily, with the help of David, it was far from a circus. David and my team agreed on the best production procedures to make it a success. Running orders and sound checks were readily agreed. They do say that a bad rehearsal leads to a successful show. And so it proved to be for 'Search'.

The final of the competition went like a dream. David was the consummate professional. He helped make the evening a tremendous success. We all enjoyed working with him, he is so cool. He took control and succeeded in steering the contest to a rock music final to be proud of.

His loyal gang of fans followed him everywhere. We allowed a handful of this colourful group to the after show party. Many of the female fans were fanny fanatics themselves, several being bi sexual. These girls were fun. One minute they were snogging me and then Emma, my girlfriend. We both had so much fun that night at the Lyceum that we did not know if we were going or coming.

Melody Maker's 'Search' succeeded

beyond my wildest dreams. The word spread and we quickly expanded our business. Bookings poured in from many more colleges and universities. College Ents had at last achieved the publicity and fame that I had always craved. It had taken many eventful years, some of which were on the brink of bankruptcy. I starved sometimes to pay the phone bill. No phone, no business.

David's first album for RCA was Hunky Dory. Hunky Dory means that everything is ok, fine and satisfactory. That positive wash of publicity splashed success all over us. Life was Hunky Dory. Hunky Dorey originates from the United States via strong Irish influence. It came to prominence in a minstrel song called 'Limerick Races'.

'Hunkey Dorey' As sung by Christy's Minstrels.
"Limerick Races "
'One of the boys am I,
That always am in clover;
With spirits light and high,
'Tis well I'm in my glory;
With your smiling faces round known all over.
Am always to be found, A singing I'm hunkey dorey.'

David Bowie was genuinely Hunky Dory with all of my staff. We all agreed that David was class.

First Class.

World Class.

THE CHILDREN THAT TIME FORGOT

"The most unusual book of the year"
— *Derek Naylor, Yorkshire Evening Post*

Peter and Mary Harrison

#TRACK 5
-THE CHILDREN THAT TIME FORGOT-

Mary got the idea for the book when she was feeding our youngest son Christopher Leon Harrison. He was a tiny baby and started picking at a floral design on the bed cover. He seemed to want to talk to her about the flowers. Mary was intrigued, she asked other mothers about their experiences.

Mary used the word 'odd' in her letter published in Woman's Own. It was the word 'odd' that started the flow of letters. A bemused Mary was reading letters about small children 'who had lived before'. Mary did not expect a response of that nature. She was overwhelmed and convinced me to start researching the stories.

We had an auction for the book via our agent. The first edition of the book was published by Futura, a Robert Maxwell company. Michael Sellers' book "P.S. I Love You", about his super star father, was published by Maxwell at the same time. Michael was miffed because we received exactly the same advance that he got. He was the son of a star, we were just unknown working journalists and authors.

When the book was published Mary toured TV

and radio stations throughout the UK. I visited all the book shop managers to promote the book. Later, a grown up Christopher became Mary's media assistant. As did my other wonderful son, Peter Antony. Paul and Philip were always there to give us support. Four sons - four gems.

Mary was employed, for some years, by LBC radio as their psychic consultant. She worked well with the show's host, Peter Murray. Pete was the definitive broadcasting professional. Some forty years earlier Pete had hosted "6.5 Special" produced by my TV producer hero Jack Good. Serendipity.

Our book is published in USA, Canada, Japan, France, Netherlands, UK & Ireland (Five reprints). It has recently been republished by Amazon, it is part of our "Paranormal Trilogy". The other two titles that make up the Trilogy: "Mystic Forces" and "Spinechiller". It's available to download from Amazon on KINDLE.

An American woman who lost her baby was so distressed that she considered suicide.

Someone gave her the American Berkeley edition of 'The Children that Time Forgot'.

Tracii says that reading "T C T T F" saved her life.

Heart saver.   By tracii - This is her review.

"My friend found this book laying on the bottom of the floor of the PX at his army base. He still isn't sure why he bought it but it saved my life. My son, Marcus, had just passed away and I was having a really hard time with his passing. I couldn't find any reason to stay here. I was going to go be with my son. Until this book!!
Chris sent me the book, but it took me over two weeks to pick it up, once I did I never put it down. I cried so hard while reading it. It made me realize that he was fine and that it wasn't my fault. Now 10 years later after that night, I'm happily married and we're trying for a baby. This book IS a life saver. THANK-YOU."

Here is the start of the first story from 'The Children That Time Forgot'.

"Kathleen, Nicola's mother, is convinced her Child has lived before. The strange story began when Nicola was given a pullalong toy dog on her second birthday. The child got very excited as she told her mother, 'I'll call it Muff, the same as the other dog I had before.' Kathleen laughed at what she thought was the overactive imagination of her little girl. She played along with the child's game of make-believe and agreed that Muff was a lovely name for her little toy dog. As the days went on Kathleen noticed that Nicola became engrossed with Muff and continually asked her toy dog if he could remember various incidents and experiences that they were supposed to have shared in the past. Assuming that it was all just a childish fantasy, Kathleen attached no importance to her daughter's so-called reminiscences, until suddenly Nicola asked her mother a strange question which made Kathleen stop and think. Being unusually articulate for her age Nicola asked her mother, 'Why am I a little girl mummy? Why am I not a boy as I was before?' When Kathleen asked Nicola what she meant, she answered, 'My other mummy was called Mrs Benson, I was a boy and I played with Muff.'

This remark left Kathleen puzzled, especially the reference to a Mrs Benson. Nicola did not know anyone called Mrs Benson and, in fact, the name was not of anyone known to the family.

As the references to what Nicola had done 'before' became more and more frequent Kathleen was forced to take note of what her daughter was saying, as the child never varied her story, even slightly.

Nicola insisted that she used to be a boy, and although she could not remember her Christian name she knew her second name had been Benson. And her mother had been known as Mrs Benson and her mother's first name had been something like Elspeth or Elsie. She was certain that she had lived near Haworth and that she had had two sisters and of course her pet dog Muff.

She remembers that her father worked on the railway and that they lived in a little house near the railway lines. She described the house in detail to her mother. 'It was grey stone in the middle of four houses joined together in a row. There were lots of fields at the back where I used to play with Muff.' Nicola tells that how her mother wore a long skirt: 'It was like a kind of pinny just like the one that my doll wears.' She recalls how her mother wore her hair all tied up.

Her father wore big heavy boots and for some reason which Nicola has refused to talk about, she did not like her father, Nicola recalls that he had a dirty black face.

Because Nicola's story was so consistent Kathleen decided to take her daughter to Haworth to endeavour to confirm the story.

On the way they got lost and Nicola turned to her mother and said, 'I know the way because Muff and I used to walk around here.'

They soon walked past four old grey-stone terraced houses exactly as Nicola had previously described.

They were on the precise spot where the child predicted they would be."

#TRACK 6
-BRIXTON BOY CALLING-

My mother took me shopping to Brixton market. While pushing me in the pram down Brixton Hill towards the market there was an air raid warning. As we reached the market our Brixton Hill home took a direct hit from a German bomb. My mother had decided, on a whim, to go on a shopping expedition to Brixton market on that fateful afternoon. Thanks mum, you're a lifesaver!

What would we do without feminine intuition? Good job it wasn't raining or I'd be DEAD. Countless lives would have been affected. Many would not exist including my amazing and wonderful children, my grandchildren or my future… ad infinitum.

Life was tough enough and then I lost my adorable mother. She quite suddenly passed away, dying of polio. I was seven.

Dad was put under immense pressure to have
us adopted or fostered. But he was courageous.
He never gave in to family, friends or the authorities. We survived as a family.

My father was always a caring and loving father to me and my lovely sister.

Aged five I went to infants' school in Brixton. Effra Parade, next to Railton Road, was the school. The first West Indian families started arriving here soon after, around 1947 – 1950. I encouraged my young classmates to be welcoming. We greeted these lovely kids with open arms. They were fun, friendly and positive. Warm sunny smiles. No problem.

Why *some* of the third and fourth generations of these people have become surly, negative, knife wielding individuals defeats me. Maybe they feel hard done by. Could be because they live in Brixton or other deprived areas. Perhaps the reason is because they resent growing up on hardnosed council estates. I grew up on one and survived without carrying a knife, or smoking hashish. Or should that be hashit!
These days it is mixed with motor oil to increase the profit. It is then marketed under a new name, CONDENSED. Condensed SHIT!

Many of the guys who push/ sell / courier drugs are resourceful, inventive, cunning and determined. Like many business people they construct a model plan and then successfully process it. If they transferred these undoubted skills to legit business they'd make a fortune and in the process save precious lives, and much individual and family heartache. I know, I've been acutely affected.

Dad was on a low wage of £8.00 [Eight] per week plus 1% of sales. I was in the grammar stream at school but wanted to get out into the big wide world. I immediately got a job (It was much easier back then) as a runner at ITV, with Associated Rediffusion at TV House, Kingsway. London. I eventually succeeded and became the first film cameraman / editor trainee at ITV.

Later I thought about the competition on that ladder to TV management achievement. I had never been to university, so I thought it best to move on. Things were changing fast in TV and beyond, 'only graduates need apply'.

I could not bring myself to tell dad that I had left this 'dream' TV job. He was proud that I was employed by ITV.

One programme I worked on with Dan Farson was called "Success Story". It featured a legendary champion racehorse. Dad was delighted and beside himself knowing that I was in the crew that was going to film the horse, Hyperion. The stallion was a superstar.

When I eventually summed up the courage to tell him he was upset and said I'd never get another job 'In a month of Sundays'. I said I'd be working again before Monday.

He laughed through his frustration. But I did just that. I got a job at Billy Smart's Circus on Clapham Common. I was breakfast cook, making porridge for the clowns. They were an ungrateful bunch of unshaven, miserable and grumpy bastards.

When I cheerfully asked who would like more of my tasty porridge they just gave mumbled grunts. I lived in a flee infested gipsy caravan on the common. But I found it enlightening when I heard about the infamous tales of sexual infidelities. The notorious one being the affair between the disfigured lion tamer and the attractive married trapeze artiste.

It was a long hard journey from the worst sink estate in Brixton to owning and managing a business in Piccadilly.
Even homeless people refused council accommodation on my Brixton estate. I wanted away from the gangs , guns, drugs and bad karma. I was ambitious and wanted out… Thankfully I soon became part of the legendary 60's crowd. We were all caught up in those hedonistic days. It was a time of fresh ideas, original design, inventive creation for the young and gifted, both black and white.

I truly believe that this was a most distinctive era. In terms of innovation, creativity and speed of discovery this 'Popular Revolution' was superior to anything that had gone before. We also witnessed the birth of the white heat of technology

It was a period of high energy and new opportunities. There was a constant buzz of excitement in the 1960's. Come with me and witness that era. During this chapter let us travel back in a time machine and share that period of magic and wonderment.

And Brixton market has always been an exciting place of adventure for me. The day that bomb exploded proved to be a lifesaving one too. Fate, destiny, fortune or chance?

Mum, dad and I lived at 100 Arodene Road, Brixton Hill, south London. My lovely sister, Jane Frances, was not born until after the war in 1947. We lived in the hut when she was born.

My father worked for Mullards. Mullard Limited was a British manufacturer of electronic components. The Mullard Radio Valve Co. Ltd. of Southfields, London. Dad was in a protected defence job, he was a mechanical engineer. I did not inherit any of his practical skills. He could take a watch to pieces and rebuild it again within a short period of time.

I am a negotiator, salesperson and businessman. I make no excuses for that fact. I enjoyed using my skills to further my various business projects and trading ventures.

See all my many jobs at the end of this chapter. And after leaving AR-TV at 17 I was privileged to have experienced a variety of jobs. And then later to live a full and wonderful life with Mary, a devoted and loving wife and mother. I am also lucky to have a guardian angel as my everlasting minder.

After the war, the house in Arodene Road was completely rebuilt; it almost exactly matched the adjacent houses that survived. However, if you inspect it carefully you will see that the rebuilt house is slightly 'off colour' to the surrounding houses that endured Hitler's bomb. The evidence is there to see, for family members to witness.

Back to my beloved Brixton market

of my childhood...The fat, cheery faced carrier bag man, with dozens of brown paper shopping bags looped on both arms, standing under the arched bridge in Brixton Station Road. His market cries were sung in a singsong rhythm, they were legendry. "CARR-I-ER BAGS! Get your Carr-i-er bag here. Strong carr-i-er bags, only tuppence each!"

Across the road, the Granville arcade contained rows of small shops that sold products from around the world.
As they do today. My favourite was the pet shop, although it always had that pungent, manky 'animal' smell. On display was a colourful parrot chirping to all potential punters, "Morning! Morning! Don't be fright! " Oh, how I desperately wanted to have that parrot as my new best friend on my shoulder, in my home - the hut.

After we were bombed out, we were rehoused in that Nissen hut on wasteland at the bottom of Tulse Hill. We had an outside toilet and no bath, just cold water. A Nissen hut is a prefabricated steel structure made from a half-cylindrical skin of corrugated steel, used extensively during World War II.

Along Atlantic Avenue there were many butchers' shops vying for trade. Some staying open until late, unusual in those days. They sold a variety of low quality meats to the Brixton lower classes. I can tell you from experience, the cheapest meats were impossible to eat. You just chewed and chewed, and then spat the 'rubbery remains' out.

Some of the meat varieties on offer were appropriate for that austere post war period: Pigeons, horseflesh and rabbits. That was luxury compared with some of the meat products I had to endure. The most popular Brixton butcher was always trying it on with his female customers. Winking and saying that he had a 'special cut' just for them. He regularly unhygienically snacked on corned beef slices with dirty hands. He chewed his corned beef at the same time as serving his 'lovely ladies' and taking their money. They paid him with their various pre-decimalization coins.

Searching in their purses for 'brown' pennies, 'golden' three-pennybits, 'silver' sixpences and shillings. Yes, those *were* the days when every *penny* counted.

Bustling past the jaunty stallholders, their loud voices rising above the general chitter chatter of the market. The green grocers shouted the loudest. "Five apples for a tanner (Sixpence 6d = 2 1/2p). Ten oranges for a bob (One shilling 1/- = 5p) and, oh yeah, I just got some pomegranates in from India. No madam I said India not Cowboys and Indians."

Further down Electric Avenue you passed the Rupp's stylish florist shop. An abundance of colourful cut flowers exuding a fragrance that robustly masked the odious market smells. Rupp's had much fine greenery with its pot plants, small trees and shrubbery. A world of natural and magnificent vibrant colours. Rupp's was a class act amongst the second billers.

At the end of that row of shops, you arrive at the ever-popular pie and mash shop. Its delicious fare included traditional jellied eels. The vendor took much delight in showing off his cutting and chopping skills.

Taking a live eel, he rapidly chopped it into little pieces with his bloodied sharp knife. Those little eel pieces wriggled for a short period of nervous existence, as if holding onto dear life itself. All to no avail because they were instantly mixed with jelly and with one gulp ended up in someone's belly. Very tasty!

And of course my own contribution…at the age of 17 I opened a bookshop in a new Brixton shopping arcade. Nobody wanted my cheap and cheerful paperbacks so it closed within a week. Soon to become part of the new Brixton underground station.

Later, still in my teens, I had a stall in Brixton market selling ex jukebox records. I also sold them in The Cut, Waterloo and in Choumert Road, Peckham, *SE15. The business was called Peter Harrison's Record Cabin.* It was in the autumn / winter / spring of 1958/59.

The market inspectors in Peckham and Brixton were kind to me. But the nasty inspector in The Cut took a dislike to me. Did he think I was a Kosher Arsenal fan or something? He used to place my stall at the bottom of 'Cold Blow Lane', near Waterloo station. It was freezing.

Because the vinyl 45 rpm records were ex juke box they all had large holes in the middle. To enable the records to be played on a record player a 'spider' had to be fitted. The 'spider' enabled the record to fit on the spindle on the record player. When I had a sale I always fitted the 'spider' for the customer. On a couple of occasions at The Cut my hands were so cold I could not fit the spider. I lost some sales due to that nasty market inspector placing my stall next to Cold Blow lane.

And in Peckham I almost had a fatal accident. I pulled the record cabin down a hill towards my market pitch. The problem was the road was covered with ice and snow. The unwieldy 'record cabin' stall on wheels pushed me towards the heavy traffic in Peckham High Street. I was being propelled towards instant death. I survived by diverting the stall into the wall of a terraced house. I was bruised, battered, cold and upset but still alive to fight another day.

My best jukebox sellers were Elvis Presley, Jan & Dean (Surfing sound) and Jackie Wilson. I also acquired some pre-war jazz recordings. I sold them to a jazz fanatic for a good profit. I enjoyed a decent meal that day. Sometimes I didn't eat until I sold a record. Hard times, warm memories.

One of the few good things about the fifties was the coming of the Lord of Rock'n'Roll, Elvis Presley. He generated music that had excitement, dynamism and energy. 'Before Elvis there was nothing.' (John Lennon and me)

In the sixties, everyone was getting on the musical bandwagon. Newspaper publishers were making a mint with pop music papers, Merseybeat, Disc, New Record Mirror, Melody Maker and New Musical Express. Only one survives.

The Melody Maker was a little grander than the 'pop music' papers. It was the weekly for the Jazz and serious 'rock' fraternity. It came in at the quality end of the market. Its articles were about American musicians, big bands and 'serious' rock groups rather than popcorn groups. The MM appealed to an educated class of music connoisseurs, being au fait with all aspects of their precious hobby. The pop fans were considered plebs, skipping from one music craze to another at the flick of a kiss curl.

One of the reasons I survived the tough early days, as a rock music agent, was because of my shift work at the cinema. I was employed as an usher, I was later promoted to 'Chief of Staff'.

The shifts meant I could work to suit my agency hours, from 1pm to 3-30pm then 6-30pm till the close of the show at 11pm. This allowed me to work in the office in the mornings and then again after 3-30pm. To save time I would pull my own trousers over the usher uniform trousers and literally run to my office in Archer Street. I could not afford to miss a single booking.

Later I arranged for a telephone answering company, T.A.S. based in Wardour Street, to answer my phone after three or four rings.
"Mr. Harrison is in a meeting at present. Can I take a message please?"

Once I had acquired several agency clients I was asked where I was between 1pm to 3.30pm. The cinema had to remain a secret, due to credibility, so I lied and said I attended business lunches.

What I was actually doing was touting for business in Leicester Square. Part of the job was to bark out our cartoon wares to the passing trade. "Bugs Bunny, Road Runner and Daffy Duck…" I roared, "…Only half a crown. Shows are continuous from eleven to eleven." Half a crown was two shillings & six pence - Twelve and a half pence.

When I came on duty at 1pm I'd say

good afternoon to Betty, the vivacious cashier. A lovely Jewish woman whom I had a crush on.

The toffee-nosed lady in the confectionary kiosk was very English, properly spoken, very twee and she wore evening gloves when she served. Shop assistants in some of the big stores in the West End were made to wear gloves when serving. This was to prevent the common shop girl's hand touching the hand of the all important customer. What bunkum!

Anyway, I would come on at 1pm and walk around. I would smile and be cheery. I would then start shouting to the crowds in Leicester Square, selling my wares, Bugs Bunny, Daffy Duck, and Road Runner etc.
I would then look up at the big clock on the Automobile Association building on the other corner of Leicester Square and almost scream. It was only a few minutes past one o'clock.

I would have to stand there shouting about Bugs bloody Bunny until THREE THIRTY PM! It was so frustrating because all I wanted to do was to be booking my groups.

Think of all that important agency business I was missing whilst working for John Cohen of JC cinemas (Jaycee). I would sometimes run across the square to the phone box and make a call to book a band. Why I never got sacked I will never know. But I did eventually sail close to the wind for a very different reason. The usherettes. They were drop dead gorgeous. I went weak just looking at them. There was a very special one called Jan. And we had an affair.

At the age of fourteen, long before I left school, I wrote to Lloyd Williams at AR-TV, TV House, Kingsway. I had read an article about him in the TV TIMES. The story was headed 'The Man with Four Phones'.

Lloyd was the Assistant Controller of Programmes (Production). I asked him if he had any jobs because I was dying to work in television production.

Obviously Lloyd didn't realise that I had not passed any GCE exams. Lloyd's secretary said, 'Not to worry. We'll definitely find you a job as a runner / post boy.' And so it came to pass that I left school in 1956 and went to work for Associated Rediffusion TV.

My heart was thumping in anticipation as I set off for my first day at TV House. Kingsway, London. WC2. I was employed in the post room. It was a new exciting experience for me. Being a sheltered council school boy, as opposed to a knowledgeable public school boy, I was surprised by the number of gay men working in TV House.

My manager in the post room was Bert Short. An old fashioned and courteous little man. He raised his hat to the ladies and spoke impeccable English. Although he was in fact of ethnic origin with a dark skin.

Bert's assistant was a right little darling. John Pullen was a Sweetie Pie. He didn't just display the fact that he was queer (The word 'gay' in those days meant 'being carefree and happy') he flaunted it. He stood about five foot seven and had peroxide hair. He spoke with a pronounced effeminate inflection and was in the Kenneth Williams mould. But not quite as waspish as Ken. John was a bundle of fun and was never a threat to us boys. We liked working with him because he was a laugh. He lived with a Stevedore in Gravesend.

Our senior boy was John Reardon. John's father had worked for Movietone News. So he was already familiar with the industry. He was a nice chap but a bit wrapped up in himself. He was called up to National Service and served in Germany. He became batman / P.A. to the Commanding Officer.

I was too young for National Service. Thank God for that. I didn't fancy being shouted at by a Sergeant Major and living with a bunch of 'hairy strangers'. Especially those who supported The Busby Babes.

John went on to become a famous TV director. For many years he directed 'London's Burning' for London Weekend Television.

Nearly all of the boys working with me applied for the two traineeships, the apprentice places. They all wanted to be a TV cameraman. The traineeships had been created after negotiations between AR-TV and the film union ACTT (now BECTU). I was interviewed by five 'bigwigs', including Ted Lloyd, Head of Film Cameras, Commander Robert Everett, Head of Programme Services. The three others included Head of Special Projects. He later had a nervous breakdown, he couldn't cope with the pressures of TV management.

The one question I can remember was, "Can you mend a fuse?" I answered honestly, "My dad does all that but I'm sure I could if I needed to."

I was chosen as Assistant Film Cameraman (Trainee). The top job that everyone wanted.

Michael Tucker, eight O Levels on his CV, became Assistant Sound Engineer (Trainee)

I was never technically gifted but I worked hard to master the challenge. I practiced and practiced at changing the film for the 16mm camera. It had to be carried out 'blind' and by touch in a black changing bag. I eventually acquired the skill.

The film we used was either Tri-X or HPS. My other key job was to be an efficient clapper boy, 'Scene five, Take two'. I also had to mark the record card showing if the shot was a 'Take' or 'U/S'.

On one occasion I got chalk dust on film star George Sanders suit. He asked for a retake and requested that the clapper boy stands away from him. What a poser!

The cameras were 16mm Arriflex. It was rumoured that Orson Welles had negotiated the sales to AR-TV. The story goes that he then agreed to perform in and produce a series of programmes for the fledgling ITV Company.

There were four two man camera

crews. The lighting cameraman was also the operator.

The assistant was the focus puller / clapper boy. We also had a 'grips' called Ernie. He had worked with Alfred Hitchcock. He educated me with stories about Hitchcock, film stars and the sexual adventures of Dan Farson, AR-TV's star interviewer.

I went on some exciting and novel camera shoots. We filmed for the new schools programmes, for the current affairs 'This Week' and many other captivating programmes. They used my voice on the very first school's programme. I had to say, 'Fruit. Wonderful fruit.' There were several takes, the dubbing guys has been drinking.

On one occasion we went to a location near the National Portrait Gallery. We set up a pitch and filmed the interviewer giving away one pound notes. The experiment went to plan, everyone ran away. I worked mainly with Adrian Cooper and Harry Hart.

The other two cameramen were Gil

Knight, soon to retire, and Ricky Balance. Ricky didn't like me for some reason. I certainly did not rate him and kept out of his way.

Adrian and Harry were always helpful, patient and kind. They both trained me in all the correct filmic procedures.

Years later Adrian booked some actors from my Artistes International agency. One of the actors was the talented Nadim Sawahla. He appeared in ITV's 'Sexton Blake' with Laurence Payne.

Adrian was always good to me. As well as booking my actors, he gifted me some TV songs to publish. Later I was in dispute with Thames TV about publishing payments. I won and Thames TV sent me a royalty cheque for one thousand pounds.

Adrian was director for the hit comedy series, 'Do Not Adjust Your Set'. The series starred Eric Idle, Michael Palin, Terry Jones and my old adversary Viv Stanshall. On Christmas Day 1968 the title was:

'Do Not Adjust Your Stocking.'

I will always be grateful to Adrian. R I P Adrian. Born: October 22, 1929 in Brighton, East Sussex, Died: January 30, 2008 (age 78) in Dinan, Côtes-d'Armor, France

As a trainee cameraman my main work was on the Dan Farson series of programmes, directed by Rollo Gamble. Another great guy to work with, he later appeared in an episode of 'Dr.Who'.

Rollo featured me in one of the programmes. It was the 'People In Trouble' series. I was in the 'Unmarried Mothers' programme. They wanted a teenager's view of unmarried sex. I did not want to upset dad, so when interviewed by Dan I said it was wrong. As dad sat there watching the programme he smiled when he heard me giving the 'correct' answer.

Dan was very professional but a bit aloof. He always drank his gin and tonic alone in the Saloon Bar. While all the crew drank pints of beer in the Public Bar.

On one occasion I was filming outside at night near Westminster Bridge. I mixed up the film and put HPS in the camera instead of TRI-X. The film lab made a report to Adrian and our boss, Ted Lloyd. In the event my 'mistake' saved the shot. If it had been shot on TRI-X it would have not shown up on the print. That was a stroke of luck.
The film sequence was urgently needed for an important programme.
It could have easily been curtains for me.

On another occasion we went to Manchester and filmed an interview with 'Taste of Honey' author Shelagh Delaney. Although she was older than me we got on really well. She took me to her window overlooking a canal. She said, 'At least one child a week drowns in that.' I felt an icy chill run through me because she was so matter of fact about it.

I did some film editing with the legendry Charlie Squires. It was always hectic in the film editing section on the eighth floor. There always seemed to be an air of panic to get the film sequences completed on time for tight production schedules. Sometimes Charlie would work through the night to meet the deadlines.

I was also in the film library. Very measured and sedate. I liked the orderly process of the department. I'd get a phone call from a programme director, 'Larry, get me all your shots of Big Ben striking nine pm.' I'd then show him all the library film on the 'moviola' machine. I liked the job but it was not in my long term plans. The library boss, John Mountford, saw my apprehension about staying at TV House. He was very kind and said, 'Don't worry, you will find success.'

When I eventually left TV House it was a great culture shock. One minute I was enjoying cocktail cigarettes with Fanny and Johnny Cradock (The Celebrity Chefs), the next I was breaking up cars on a Camberwell bomb site.

When I left AR-TV I was still only 17. I then experienced several employment adventures. These included:

* Breakfast cook at Billy Smart's Circus, Clapham Common.

* General Dealer on the Streets of London. A Rag 'n' Bone man buying and selling clothes, trinkets and household items. I wanted a horse and cart but had to make do with a hand cart and a handbell. I felt like a character from Monty Python, 'Bring out your dead'

* I was a 'car breaker' on a bomb site in Camberwell. I hated it and left after a few days.

* Market Record Retailer - (Peter Harrison's Record Cabin) in Brixton, Peckham and Lower Marsh / The Cut, Waterloo.

*Jukebox Record Selector for Soho Coffee Bars (Including famous 2 I's) - Jukebox Distributors Ltd Company based in Wardour Street, opposite 'The George' pub.

*Asst. Exploitation Manager ~ Triumph Records, Based in Holloway road, North London.

*Asst. Sales Manager ~ Triumph Records

*Assistant to Record Producer Joe Meek 'TELSTAR'

Having no capital, aged eighteen, I made an appointment to see our friendly bank manager at Barclay's, Brixton.

He wished me luck then showed me the door. This self-important git, with a watch chain hanging from his waist coat, had no idea about a young person's requirements. He lived in a class ridden bubble with other members of the bowler hatted brigade.

All these upper middle class snoots talking down to the working man and woman, people who craved to create a business of their own. One thing about multi racialism is that the class nonsense I endured has all but diminished.

Except that the monarchy lingers. They represent hypocrisy and greed of the highest order. Who needs castles, palaces and treasure chests full of gold? It is incongruous to accept their rich lifestyle against that of sick and starving children throughout the world. When are the great British public going to wake up?

Monarchy is a great big con. Let the punk rock song "God Save The Queen" ring out loud and clear across the land. Change must rid us of this 'fascist regime'.

But I do believe in the King of Kings. A wonderful teacher of goodness and a part time carpenter. He has saved my life.

It was because of His 'miracle' that I can still work a sixteen hour day, writing scripts and books. I smoked cigarettes since I was eight {Woodbines}. I really did enjoy smoking all through my teenage years. On my 20th birthday I was waiting for the night bus at Charing Cross Embankment. An evangelist approached me and asked what I was going to give up for Jesus. I said, 'Nothing'. He suggested I give up smoking. I immediately stamped out my cigarette {Senior Service} and never smoked again.

After I sold the agency in the early 1970's I became a touring variety and show producer. My most successful show starred Jimmy Shand and his band.

"Scottish Music Hall" was very popular. We sold out in every venue, the length and breadth of Britain. Even the Colston Hall, Bristol was packed. Jimmy was a lovely, honest and straightforward man. And I adored the Scottish music he and his band played. He was knighted on his death bed.

When on tour in Inverness, Mary and I were told that The Loch Ness Monster really does exist. According to the locals it is a gigantic eel. The area has a history of monster like eels in their Lochs.

I produced several other shows, including one at that magnificent theatre in Bradford, the Alhambra. It was called, "A Wee Drop of Scotch."

One of my favourite acts was Mrs. Shufflewick, the drag queen. The first and best 'drag' act in town. 'She' was supreme.

Talented Rex Jamieson, from Camden, played her ladyship.

Her act was rude, offensive and very funny.

On my thirtieth birthday, the 9th December, I produced (With Mary) "Golden Memories" starring Reg 'Confidentially' Dixon and Mrs.Shufflewick.

Here is a quote from my YouTube page about that performance.

<u>"A lovely lovely GAL!</u>

I produced REX as SHUFF for many of my variety shows. On one occasion 'she' was second on the bill to Reg "Confidentially" Dixon.Reg ran up to me, just before curtain up, and said, 'Peter, you must put Shuff on last – I cannot possibly follow his outrageous act.'

So although my show "Golden Memories" had Reg at the top of the bill on all the posters, Shuff was star billing on this occasion. SHUFF was always on top. His comic timing was immaculate.
Larry Peter Harrison"

Mary *and I loved Shuff. We enjoyed many a laugh with Shuff over a glass or three of Guinness.*

We produced a show in Preston called 'Tribute to Robert Burns' with Kenneth McKellar. *See the poster in the photos section.* He was a superb singer of the traditional songs of Scotland, including all Burns' songs. His rendition of the Burns' classic, 'My Love Is Like A Red Red Rose' was magnificent.

The show sold out because we had young Neil Reid on the bill. At that time he was No. 1 in the charts with 'Mother of Mine'. Tickets became so scarce that we couldn't squeeze the Town Dignitaries in to see it. There was no 'mayor' room. That was my brother in law's joke, don't blame me. Some shows made money and others lost.

My big disaster was "Big Band Cavalcade" at The Queen's Theatre, Margate in the summer of 1971. The only thing that didn't go wrong at that time was my budding romance with my gorgeous best friend.

I returned to Archer Street, London where the agency came to my financial rescue. It always paid for my costly failures. The music agency was hard work but always flourished financially. But I was always searching for extra income streams via various entertainment and promotions.

I formed a partnership with Brunel University and we promoted Sunday concerts at the Lyceum in the Strand. The first week made good money. The following week we thought we'd make a killing with The Fairport Convention. It snowed and we lost everything.

In 1967 I started promoting West Indian dance events in the Town Halls in Ealing and Acton. I employed an excellent West Indian band called the Maroons. They were popular with the British Caribbean audience . These dance promotions always made a profit. But I had to keep my head down, they didn't like a 'Whitey' organising their entertainment.

My friend Alan Jacobs was saving to go back to Australia. I wanted to help him financially so I paid him to assist. All the thanks he got was a threatening knife to the throat from

a member of the audience.
But Alan did eventually return to the land that he loves.

Employment Profile of the AUTHOR:

TEENAGE YEARS & EARLY 20's:

*Post Boy/Runner Associated Rediffusion,
TV HOUSE, Kingsway.

*Senior Post Boy / Runner ~ AR-TV.

*Trainee/Apprentice Film Cameraman

*Breakfast Cook in Circus ~ Billy Smart.

*General Dealer ~ The Streets of London.
*Record Retailer ~ (Peter Harrison's Record Cabin) Markets in Brixton, Peckham and Lower Marsh / The Cut, Waterloo.

*Record Selector for Soho Coffee Bars.

*Asst. Exploitation Manager.
*Asst. Sales Manager ~ Triumph

Records.
*Assistant to Record Producer Joe Meek.

*Chief of Staff, J C Cinema, Leicester Sq.

*Rock Music Agent ~ C E O Star Attractions

MID to LATE 20's:

*Man. Director: College Entertainments Ltd.
Artistes International & Star Attractions.

*Promoter West Indian dances. W. London.

*Producer of Tribute to Robert Burns.

*Producer of Big Band Cavalcade.

*Producer of touring show 'Scottish Music Hall' ~with Jimmy Shand & his band.

*Producer of 'Wee Drop Of Scotch' at Bradford Alhambra.

*Producer of 'Music Hall' ~ London

venues.
*Producer of 'Golden Memories' Variety Show with Reg Dixon / Mrs.Shufflewick.

THIRTIES & FORTIES + :

*Author with Mary of best seller 'The Children That Time Forgot'.

The book has sold all over the world, including Japan.

*Radio Presenter/Producer for Central Office of Information. Freelance reporter for BBC Radio London.

Business Ventures

Bought and developed Newsagents in Bournemouth - 'Harrison News'. *I worked from 6am to 9pm 7 days a week – Grueling !*

Bought and developed Video shop, Carshalton 'Movieland'. Great fun.

Bought, developed and sold property in Northampton. In the right place and at the right time. Prices soaring.

C E O of 'Mortgage Centre UK Ltd' in Wellingborough. Many successful years.

It was a flourishing business then interest rates shot through the roof. Our family suffered, it was devastating.

Mortgages plentiful until Major Minor ruined our lives.

INTERNATIONAL PRESS-CUTTING BUREAU
224-236 Walworth Road,
London SE17 1JE

Extract from
Western Mail, Cardiff.

- 3 MAR 1990

Castle venue for TV series exploring psychic events

By RICHARD PAYTON

A TELEVISION series which tries to explain the unexplained — ghosts, premonitions, and out of body experiences was recorded at Cardiff Castle yesterday.

Hosted by David Frost, the series will have a different international guest star every week.

It aims to give a Christian view of the unexplained and steers clear completely of the occult.

Filmed in the Banqueting Hall of the castle, the programme, called *Night Visitors*, will feature people talking about their out of body experiences.

Mr Peter Harrison, writer on psychic happenings, and the series creator, said the whole aim of *Night Visitors* was to explain the unexplained.

In the first episode actress Sian Phillips will tell a ghost story and Toyah Wilcox and Lyndsey De Paul will talk about their own encounters with the unexplained.

Mr Harrison said he felt that a lot of people would have had out of body experiences, so the programme would talk directly to them.

"When my wife Mary was working for LBC in London as a psychic agony aunt, she had a lot of calls from people who said they had left their bodies, looked back at themselves and then returned to their bodies again," he said.

Mr Harrison said that during the 1980s there had been a mushrooming interest in the unexplained.

The Rev. Graham St John-Willey, a congregational minister from Northampton, will also be on the programme talking about his out of body experience. Mr Harrison said this showed that the idea had the support of Christians.

The programme, made by Wyvern Rogers Television, is to be shown on HTV, but Mr Harrison said he thought it would be bought by an American network.

In her recently-published book called *Mystic Forces*, Mary Harrison relates a story of Cardiff motorist Derek Scott, who was involved in a road smash and taken to hospital in terrible pain.

While a nurse was fussing over him the man suddenly found himself on the ceiling looking down on his hospital bed.

He could see a yellow card stuck in the light. The card was not visible from floor level.

Mr Scott "fell" back into his body and experienced the pain again. He told the nurse about the card, which she retrieved from the light.

MARY HARRISON

(Harrison at 123 Midland Road, Wellingborough, Northants NN8 1LU.)

Mary and I were Co-Producers of 'NIGHT VISITORS' with David Frost.

Previous Publications
By Peter & Mary Harrison

"Life Before Birth"
Macdonald Futura

"The Children That Time Forgot"
Sinclair

"Mystic Forces"
Sinclair

"Spinechiller"
Sinclair

"Supernatural"
Sinclair

"Money Making Hobbies"
Sinclair

"Coins & Banknotes For Profit"
Barrie & Jenkins

"Stamp Collecting For Profit"
Barrie & Jenkins

"Make Money From Your Car"
Kaye & Ward

"Food For Love"
Jupiter

TRACK 7
POSITIVE INFLUENCES

Mary Margaret Harrison – My Beloved

My beautiful loving wife had the greatest influence on me. She was always positive. Brought up in a poor mining village, near Edinburgh. She excelled at school. She entered a school story competition. The tale was about a growing friendship between a priest and a nun. Mary told about their love for Jesus having to be greater than the love for each other. Circumstances sadly dictated the ending of the budding relationship. In the event Mary's entry was of a quality too high for the Catholic school journal. Disappointingly, it was never published.

Mary and I were great fun buddies long before any romance blossomed, really good mates. We shared the same sense of humour and always laughed at the most ridiculous things.

She came to work for me at College Entertainments Ltd. in Archer Street. She was our college co-ordinator. Mary had a PR background having worked with Bing Crosby's Irish agent. Therefore she made an ideal co-ordinator for my company. She mixed public relations with obtaining new business. She was very popular with social secretaries and their committees.

We enjoyed mixing with musicians, singers and artistes. We met them in the Archer Street pubs including The Lyric.
We also enjoyed frequenting gay pubs in Soho together. We liked the chat, the affability and the ambience. We found it thoroughly relaxing.

One magic morning I woke up and discovered that I was totally in love with my best friend. I could not live or breathe with her.

We were together for 30 years. I have to tell you that Mary excited me just as much in year 30 as in year 1. She must be looking after me otherwise I'd never survive. Mary was so bubbly, effervescent, optimistic and positive. She was a loving wife and a very caring mother, she passed over in 2002.

We all miss her so very much.

Mary Harrison

The Ladies' Man

By Mary Harrison
Based
on the life and times of Thomas Hardy

Copyright © Mary Harrison 1999

Wilfrid Harrison - My Hero father.

I must have seemed a very odd son in my father's eyes. At the age of five, I told my parents a big lie. I said that my Effra Parade school, Brixton, had singled me out as their brightest ever pupil. I was just trying to get some attention. I also stole a plastic model reindeer from the teacher's desk. I then gave it to my mother as a gift. I also brought in a knife, from our kitchen drawer, when I heard one small kid say to an even smaller kid, "I'm gonna kill you".

I'm certain that my father never predicted this infant anarchy when he first heard that my mother was pregnant. It was a surprise conception, not a planned one. However, I am very pleased they kept me in that warm, safe womb. Some members of my mother's immediate family, especially the sisters, had other merciless suggestions. They did not want my mother, Esme, throwing her life away with an unskilled seaman. She was a beautiful and very intelligent young woman in her early twenties. She had a wonderful life stretching out in front of her. My dad was a seasoned seafarer approaching his mid-thirties. He once told me that resembling 'Humphrey Bogart' made him attractive to the fairer sex.

Many suitors chased the beautiful Esme Kathleen Heath around Clapham, including one wealthy gentleman, where she lived in the large family house in Franconia Road. She grew up in Sommers Road, Brixton Hill.

Her father, Thomas Heath, was a Brixton Prison Officer and her mother, Liz, a homemaker. Grandma had no other options, she had twelve children. Although grandma was kind to me, my grandfather was distant and unfriendly. Possibly due to the status of my father. Both of my maternal grandparents were Conservatives. They owned their own house at 9, Franconia Road, Clapham, south London. I used to go around there for my weekly bath, ours was a tin bath. My grandparents paid only a few hundred pounds for this magnificent five-bedroom three story Victorian house. It is now worth in excess of £1,500,000. That's property inflation for you. This area in Clapham is now 'yuppie land' boasting high-class restaurants and wine bars.
In the days of my grandparents it was very working class. Many people were

close to the breadline. No benefits in those days. You either worked or you starved.

The pressure on my mother to have me aborted in the summer of 1941 increased. Her sister, my aunt, confessed this family secret to me. However, my father was also under pressure later for another reason. When Esme died of Infantile Paralysis (Polio) in November 1949, I was seven and my sister, Jane, was two. In those far off days it was unheard of for a single father to care for children so young.

The local community asked, 'How can a widowed man, in his early forties, be expected to be mother and father to those children and hold down a full time job?' Many people put pressure on him to have us adopted or put in an orphanage. Not only his workmates and friends at the greyhound track, but also close family members on both sides of the divide.

He was also spoken to by the do-gooders at Lambeth council and church connections. But he resisted. He decided to keep us together as a family unit. It was hard, but Jane and I recently agreed that it had worked successfully.

Local forces were powerful and all persuading. He was a courageous man to stick with his judgment. He was on his own, nobody else backed his decision.

My father was a very shy man. However, we wished he had opened up a little and told us about his life, loves and times on the high seas as a merchant sailor. His own grandfather had been a head teacher in a Yorkshire school.

But Charles, dad's father, was blown to pieces on the Somme in World War 1. His mother, Clarrie, died of a broken heart soon after that tragic event. The young Wilfrid was forced to stay with an alcoholic aunt in south London. Because his father was killed in the 'Great War', he received educational dispensation.

The law was that the State had to compensate a child orphaned by that war. He therefore gained a place at The Strand Boys Grammar School, Tulse Hill. One thing he did tell me was quite amusing. One day, at lunchtime, the children were about to eat their school lunch when no master appeared to say grace. Although it was said in Latin, the school caretaker stepped forward and said grace, in Latin. The boys laughed because they thought there's no way he could know any Latin. They concluded that he just remembered it, parrot fashion, after hearing it repeated so many times by the masters.

One of the reasons I wrote this book was because I wanted to create a link between the past and the future. One of my sons, and also a daughter, always craved information about our family history. My maternal grandfather from Clapham was going to write about his memories of the Boer war. He never got around to it, much to the disappointment of his children, my aunts and uncles.

My father, sadly, never did beguile us with tales of the high seas. Telling about the different countries and peoples he had experienced. He ran away from the alcoholic aunt aged about 15. He went to Tiger Bay in Cardiff, Wales to jump on a ship going far far away. At that age he would have been a cabin boy.

However, he did tell us three stories concerning his life on the ocean wave and also about a decision of destiny.

The first was that Rio de Janeiro was the best and most fun place on earth. The people were so warm and welcoming, especially the girls. Everyone was happy and relaxed. His previous experience was that of a tough Yorkshire farming upbringing. Stiff wing collars, pomposity and attending church twice on a Sunday. As a young boy he was castigated for giggling in church. He saw the ridiculous side of the religious costumes and rituals and just could not stop laughing.

The second story was on board ship. A black seaman was always having favours done by the ship's captain. Dad approached the black man, who was a friend, and asked him why the skipper always danced to his demands. "Because we're both Freemasons" came the surprising reply.

The third event affected all of us in the Harrison/Stewart clans. A sad, lonely and dispirited Wilfrid Binns Harrison {13th May 1907} was undecided about whether to go back to sea or stay in London. This thirty-two year old man was having something of a midlife crisis.

He was a little downcast when he said

to himself, 'If the next traffic light is red then I stay but if it is green, I go back to sea.' Thank God it was red because if it had been green then our futures would have been null, void and non-existent. A fifty fifty chance in our favour.

Thank you DAD for being my DAD.

Ain't life grand!

Jack Good–Best TV music producer ever.

Jack Good, with beard. Trevor Peacock centre. Peter left.

I first heard of Jack Good when I was still a camera/editor trainee at Associated Rediffusion. He worked for ABC TV after leaving the BBC on a point of principle. That point was that Jack wanted to produce the BBC TV programme '6.5 Special' in his own style. A style that appealed to the teenagers.

BBC TV insisted on making pottery and

talking about other hobbies. Jack wanted rock'n'roll, jazz music and jiving fun. Jack wanted ZING! His mix was music, chat and fun. He knew exactly what the teenage audience wanted. And he gave it to them via that fast moving and thrilling Rock 'n' Roll show called 'Oh Boy'. Every Saturday, live at 6.pm from Hackney Empire.

I am using an 'Oh Boy' computer mouse mat as I type this chapter. It features a photo of Jack Good, arms outstretched and mouth wide open, in front of Neville Taylor and the Cutters. On the mouse mat the first TV Times programme listing of 'Oh Boy' is reprinted below.

'New Show', Oh Boy!

An Explosion of Beat Music with Bertice Reading, Marty Wilde, Ronnie Carroll, The Dallas Boys, Cherry Wainer, The John Barry Seven, Lord Rockingham's X1, Neville Taylor and the Cutters, The Vernons Girls, Red Price and introducing Cliff Richard and the Drifters.

Musical direction by Harry Robinson,

Dance direction by Leslie Cooper,

*Script by Trevor Peacock,
Directed by Rita Gillespie,*

*Produced by JACK GOOD.
An ABC Network Production.*

I was *just seventeen* when I wrote to Jack for permission to come over to the Hackney Empire and watch the show. He was then twenty-eight years old and full of youthful enthusiasm. He replied to me immediately saying, 'Come on over, you're welcome'. I worked at TV House, Kingsway for AR-TV, from Monday to Friday so I was free on Saturdays. I attended both the afternoon rehearsals and live evening shows.

I can hardly describe the excitement running through me at that first performance I attended at the Hackney Empire.
Cliff Richard looking crisp, handsome and very confident. Marty Wilde was chatting up a beautiful girl from the show. She eventually became his wife. The Dallas Boys looked dapper in their coloured jackets. The Vernons Girls were meticulous, attractive and tuneful.

Witnessing that first dress rehearsal was exhilarating. And over in the corner of the stage Neville Taylor and his Cutters rehearsing their harmonies. Next to Red Price, on sax, was Cherry Wainer camping it up on organ.

I walked up the stairs to the balcony and sat in the centre seat. I then lit a Senior Service (untipped) cigarette and pretended to produce the show. Jack was so focused that he hardly glanced up at me in the balcony. But when he did wave at me I felt a thrill of belonging and connecting with his production. The highlight for me was when Lord Rockingham's X1 played 'Hoots Mon'.

Many years later I tried to meet up with Jack. His minders turned me away when he toured his musical. On another occasion I thought I was close but he went abroad. But I did attend his ITV production of 'Around The Beatles' in 1964. He was far too busy to meet me in those circumstances. Rita Gillespie directed. The Fab Four excelled - as per usual. They were great as were all the supporting acts.

I eventually got to meet Jack in a pub near his home in Oxfordshire. It was a great occasion for me. However, I don't think he trusted me one hundred per cent at first. He was a little defensive but when I recalled my time in TV and at the Hackney Empire he relaxed a little.

At first, he thought I was a reporter from The Times updating his eventual obituary. Then he thought that I was maybe from a tabloid investigating Elvis Presley's sex life. Nothing could have been further from the truth.

I just wanted to be in the company of this brilliant man and chat about his life in music, theatre and film. He appeared with Cary Grant and Trevor Howard in 'Father Goose' in 1964 and also had a part in an Elvis Presley movie.

After leaving AR-TV I was at career crossroads. I wrote to Jack in 1958 from my pitch in Peckham market, selling jukebox records in Choumert Road. I asked Jack for his guidance. When the postman eventually found me in the market he delivered Jack's reply. In the letter Jack advised that the future was on the high seas. He was talking about the fast developing Pirate Radio stations, prior to Radio 1. He advised me to become a pirate disc jockey. I considered the idea but finally rejected it. My life would have been very different if I had followed Jack's valued advice. Very different indeed, but for me it was a step too far. I'm a home boy.

Watching 'The Girl Can't Help It' and 'Blackboard Jungle' changed his life forever. Both films featured rock'n'roll stars performing rock'n'roll classics. Bill Hayley, Eddie Cochrane, Gene Vincent, Little Richard, The Platters etc.

The exact same thing happened to me. When I got rock'n'roll in my blood I was hooked - Forever. No cold turkey for me. That exhilarating music changed my life and my goals. It proved to be my music drug of a lifetime. I don't do the other lot.

How can an Oxford swot allow rock'n'roll to enter his life? Jack went for the elation of music, as if it were the very oxygen of life. He succeeded as a brilliant TV producer. He became an icon. Ironically, he now paints them.

I mention Jack's foresight. The following quote was made years before video recording was commercially perfected.
"It will become the standard practice for every artist to make a film of themselves performing their record. These short films will be sent to TV producers for their programmes...it

would not be a disc at all but a videotape. You would play it on your television, which would have a recorder-like attachment, which would also allow you to record your favourite TV programmes." - Jack Good, January 1959.

Jack was born in Greenford, Middlesex on 7 August 1931. Jack once told me that during the Second World War an ack ack gun continually fired near his home in Greenford. His family got used to the repetitive sound and eventually ignored it. They then only noticed the 'void' when it stopped firing.

Jack was always drawn towards drama and entertainment. He played Othello at the age of fifteen. He was also in a double act, with Trevor Peacock, at the Windmill Theatre. That famous theatre featured nude girls. I went to see the nude show a couple of times, as a kid. The girls never moved and, to me, they were incredibly boring. Some of the comedians were funny. I'm certain Jack and Trevor were hilarious.

Jack featured rocker Tommy Steele, skiffle leader Lonnie Donegan, and jazzmen Johnny Dankworth and Humphrey Lyttleton and many many more on his BBC TV show. After the BBC demanded that '6.5 special' should put the emphasise on a teenage magazine format Jack resigned. Jack joined ITV and launched *Oh Boy!* in June 1958. The programme (1958-59) became television's first true showcase for rock 'n' roll stars. Jack was instrumental in helping launch the careers of a young Cliff Richard, Marty Wilde and the wonderful Billy Fury.

I once saw Billy at the Trocedera, Elephant & Castle. Billy was a star. Billy was stupendous. His performance stays with me to this day. His 'Halfway to Paradise' is in my top ten. My wife Mary and I knew Billy's long-term girlfriend. Her name was Lee Everett and she had the same book publisher as us, Futura.

Oh Boy's dynamic parade of non-stop rock performers barely gave the screaming audience time to draw breath.

The show became a milestone in music television production. Eventually leading the way to MTV and the likes. Jack followed with *Boy Meets Girl* (ITV, 1959-60), an equally hectic sequel featuring Marty Wilde as presenter and

performer, and guests including Terry Dene, Adam Faith and Joe Brown.
Through *Boy Meets Girls* Jack was instrumental in introducing American rockers Eddie Cochran and Gene Vincent to the British public.

Jack brought many top American music stars to appear on British TV. Probably more than any other producer, then and since.

Jack is known as a pioneering TV television producer, musical theatre producer, record producer, musician, film actor and painter of icons.

To me Jack has always been a golden treasure of wisdom, guidance and genuine kindness. Thank you Jack.

Joe Meek – The innovative record producer

Before I started my rock agency I was Joe Meek's assistant at his office in Holloway Road. His 'Telstar' made number 1. I started working for Joe when I was his sales rep for Saga records. I was still only 18, having recently left AR-TV.

Saga distributed Triumph records, from

their offices based in Empire Yard, Holloway Road, north London. In January 1960, together with Barrington-Coupe, Meek founded Triumph Records. At the time Barrington-Coupe was working at SAGA records for Major Wilfred Alonzo Banks and it was the Major who provided the finance. The label very nearly had a Number 1 hit with *Angela Jones* by Michael Cox. Cox was one of the featured singers on Jack Good's TV music show *Boy Meets Girl. The* song was given massive promotion. As an independent label Triumph was at the mercy of small pressing plants, which could not, or would not, keep up with the 45 rpm vinyl sales demand.

Major Banks, the scoundrel, still owes me one hundred pounds in commission. Major Banks had called a meeting of all the reps. He challenged each one of us to break the record 'Angela Jones' by Michael Cox into the massive Broadmead electrical & record store chain. He promised us that dazzling amount of commission money (it was in those days) on the first order from Broadmead. I could have used that money to start my agency.

I succeeded in being the first rep to sell

that record into the chain. It happened like this...I was walking past the Broadmead branch in Peckham High Street and noticed the girl putting an advertising board outside the shop. It was the Hit Parade Top Twenty. I studied the list and then went inside to see the manager.

"I represent Triumph records and the official *New Musical Express* Top Twenty puts our version of the Angela Jones record at Number 16. Your adverting board shows the American version. That's wrong and I'll report it."

Immediately the manager gave me a sizable order and changed the board to read 'Angela Jones by Michael Cox'.

As mentioned, I never got that commission but I did get a promotion. I was given the position of Assistant Exploitation Manager. Promotion and Record Plugging, with manager Frank Kelly.
What a wise guy he was.

I then became the company's Assistant Sales Manager. My sales manager, Mr. Jones, was young, fresh and enthusiastic. He gave me a lift into work every day. He lived in the Brixton area.

Angela Jones made a respectable appearance in the Top Ten, but it proved Joe needed the major companies' distribution muscle to get his records into the shops when it mattered. In spite a great catalogue of Meek productions, its business results were not good. Joe was proving difficult to work with and this eventually led to the label's demise.

Joe later licensed many Triumph recordings to labels such as Top Rank and Pye. I was involved in some of the Top Rank negotiations. They were later bought out by E M I. Decades later a play was written about Joe's life entitled 'Telstar'. I took my family to see it in the West End. Afterwards I went to the stage door to meet the various actors playing the parts of people I had worked with.

The actor playing the part of Joe Meek studied me closely. I had just congratulated him on his magnificent portrayal of Joe in the West End play, of the same name, 'Telstar'. In the play, which was honest, Joe kisses Heinz, one of his stars. I told the actor that Joe never kissed me. His searching look gave his thoughts away which probably were…Well, you're not as good looking as Heinz.

Joe was part of the 'Pink Mafia'. Something I was never involved in. Some say it was akin to being a show biz freemason. If you were ambitious and wanted to be somebody in show business then being in the 'gay circle' was a definite advantageous.

Joe and Robert Stigwood linked together in the career of John Leyton. John had a number 1 hit, produced by Joe, 'Johnny Remember Me'. Robert was John Leyton's agent and manager. I found John Leyton to be a pleasant bloke and a good pro. Joe did tell me that Stigwood had constant rows with his artistes. Joe said it pissed him off. I was never witness to any of these alleged angry quarrels.

Joe once auditioned Rod Stewart. Instead of telling Rod that it was a 'pass', Joe blew a 'raspberry' in Rod's face. That was Joe all right!

A few years later Joe's depression deepened as his financial position became increasingly desperate. French composer, Jean Ledrut, accused Joe Meek of plagiarism, claiming that the tune of 'Telstar' had been copied from "La Marche d'Austerlitz", a piece from a score Ledrut had written for the 1960 film *Austerlitz*. This lawsuit meant Meek never received royalties from the record during his lifetime.

On 3 February 1967, the eighth anniversary of Buddy Holly's death, Joe killed his landlady Violet Shenton. It was a dispute about overdue rent. He then put the gun in his mouth and pulled the trigger. His head, horrifically, burnt like a candle. Joe was buried at Cemetery lodge Newent, Gloucestershire. His black granite tombstone can be found near the middle of the cemetery.

The lawsuit was eventually ruled in Joe's favour three weeks after his death in 1967. It is unlikely that Joe was aware of *Austerlitz*, as it had been released only in France at the time. Joe was a mixed up and confused man with many faults. A techie who couldn't read a note of music, but succeeded in spite of that vital liability.

He was a shining inspiration, wholly focused on his aims. He succeeded in spite of people in the business treating him like a country boy, he spoke with a soft West Country burr. However, Joe's talent always shone through.

Lloyd Williams – AR–TV

As a schoolboy, aged fourteen, I had written to Lloyd Williams at AR-TV. I had read an article about him in the TV TIMES. The story was headed 'The Man with Four Phones'. Lloyd was the Assistant Controller of Programmes (Production). I asked him if he had any jobs because I was dying to work in television production. He invited me into TV House just after my fifteenth birthday. Lloyd had faith in me and I will always be grateful to him for that.

Obviously, Lloyd didn't realise that I had not passed any GCE exams. The reason was because I was too young to take them and I would rather work at ITV than stay at school. Lloyd sent me along to AR-TV's Chief accountant Mr. J.S.Harrower. He was very pleasant, courteous and condescending to this fifteen-year-old boy. But he told me I was not educated to the standard required for a job as 'Accounts Assistant'. Lloyd's secretary said, 'Not to worry. We'll find you a job for you in the Post Room'. And so it came to pass that I left school in 1956 and went to work for Associated Rediffusion.

My heart was thumping in anticipation as I set off for my first day at TV House. Kingsway London WC2. It was a whole new exciting experience for me. My first big shock was to discover how many gays were working in TV.

My manager in the post room was Bert Short. A very old fashioned and courteous little man. He's assistant was John Pullen. He was very gay man who minced his way along.

Our senior boy was John Reardon in the Post Room. I later succeeded him in that elevated job. He was called up to National Service. I escaped it because of my age, too young at the cutoff point. John went on to become a well-respected TV director of 'London's Burning' for L W T.

Adrian Cooper – TV Director

Adrian was always there for me. When I was 16 he taught me various film camera skills. When I was 26 he booked actors from my agency for his ITV drama productions. And later he kindly gave me valuable music to publish, played on his popular ITV children's programme.

Several of my actors were cast in the George Bernard Shaw play 'Captain Brassbounds Conversion'. Adrian was my guest of honour on that first night, 18 February 1971, at the Cambridge theatre. It starred Ingrid Bergman. Ingrid and Kenneth Williams gifted me with a theatre programme signed by the entire cast.

THE DISPOSSESSED

CAN I MAKE IT THROUGH THE NIGHT?

Author/Producer: Larry Peter Harrison Music Producer : Phil Doyle

The Dispossessed

I will always appreciate the huge effort made by the cast to ensure that my play was a success.

Craig Carter, brilliant actor.
Julia Shevelova, radiates talent.
Shelley McDonald, outstanding.
Chloe Sinclair, exudes excellence.

The play was performed in April 2012 as 'Squat'.

The story tells of a young rock musician who is surviving in a Camden squat. He teams up with a local group and makes it to the top. But he becomes egotistical and demanding and loses everything.

The lead actor in 'Squat' quit before the contracted theatre run in May and June. I was left with a dreadful dilemma. Do I cancel and let the theatre down or try, in the short time available and re-cast and re-produce.

Shelley McDonald took over the lead part with distinction; Chloe Sinclair stepped in at the last moment to play the part of Golda. The play was retitled, 'The Dispossessed'.

Shakespearean director Dan Burgess, from the Globe theatre, stepped into the breach. He worked around the clock with the cast to save our play. To witness those young heroic actors work so hard was truly inspirational. Determination was their watchword.

With Dan's skillful directing the play was well received by all Camden audiences throughout the run. Also special thanks to Kate and Charlotte at The Etcetera Theatre. With their unique help we made the play a great success.

Thank you actors company for your brilliant positive attitude.

THE DISPOSSESSED

Author/Producer: Larry Peter Harrison - Director: Dan Burgess of Globe Theatre
Cast: Craig Carter - Julia Shevelova - Shelley McDonald - Chloe Sinclair

BOOK NOW
Etcetera Theatre : 265 Camden High Street : Camden Town
Tuesday 29 May to Sunday 3 June ~ 7.30 nightly ~ Sunday 6:30